SCHOLASTIC

READ & RESPOND

Bringing the best books to life in the classroom

G000058545

Planning Guide

Terms and conditions

IMPORTANT – PERMITTED USE AND WARNINGS – READ CAREFULLY BEFORE USING

Recommended system requirements:
- Windows: XP (Service Pack 3), Vista (Service Pack 2), Windows 7,
- Windows 8 and Windows 10 with 2.33GHz processor
- Mac: OS 10.6 to 10.10 with Intel Core™ Duo processor
- 1GB RAM (recommended)
- 1024 x 768 Screen resolution
- CD-ROM drive (24x speed recommended)
- Adobe Reader (version 9 recommended for Mac users)
- Microsoft Word
- Broadband internet connections (for installation and updates)

For all technical support queries (including no CD drive), please phone Scholastic Customer Services on 0845 6039091

Scholastic Education, an imprint of Scholastic Ltd
Book End, Range Road, Witney, Oxfordshire, OX29 0YD
Registered office: Westfield Road, Southam, Warwickshire CV47 0RA

www.scholastic.co.uk

1 2 3 4 5 6 7 8 9   7 8 9 0 1 2 3 4 5 6

British Library Cataloguing-in-Publication Data
A catalogue record for this book is available from the British Library.

ISBN 978-1407-16944-6

Printed and bound by Ashford Colour Press

Author Sarah Snashall
Editorial Rachel Morgan, Jenny Wilcox, Margaret Eaton, Vicky Butt
Cover and Series Design Neil Salt and Nicolle Thomas
Layout Neil Salt

Contents

Introduction

Read & Respond provides teaching ideas related to a specific children's book. The series focuses on best-loved books and brings you ways to use them to engage your class and enthuse them about reading. This book provides literacy coordinators with a suggested teaching order and structure for the *Read & Respond* series, as well as summaries about the children's books and content covered in the accompanying teacher's books. You will need copies of the children's book and the teacher's books to be able to utilise the information in this book in the classroom.

The book is broken down into year-group sections and each year is broken down into six terms, each with a suggested title to cover. This is summarised on the components charts on pages 6–8. There is a contents page at the start of each year group, showing which books are covered when. This is then followed by an overview of each book, which includes:

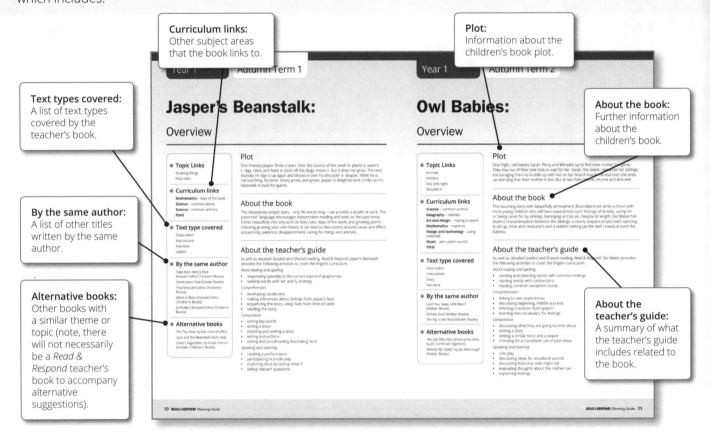

Curriculum links: Other subject areas that the book links to.

Plot: Information about the children's book plot.

Text types covered: A list of text types covered by the teacher's book.

About the book: Further information about the children's book.

By the same author: A list of other titles written by the same author.

Alternative books: Other books with a similar theme or topic (note, there will not necessarily be a *Read & Respond* teacher's book to accompany alternative suggestions).

About the teacher's guide: A summary of what the teacher's guide includes related to the book.

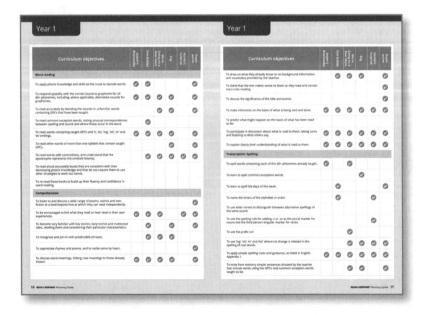

At the end of each year group, you will find a Curriculum Links grid, which shows the curriculum coverage for each *Read & Respond* title in that year group.

About the digital component

Below are brief guidance notes for using the digital component.

Getting started

Put the CD-ROM into your CD-ROM drive.

- For Windows users, the install wizard should autorun; if it fails to do so then navigate to your CD-ROM drive. Then follow the installation process.
- For Mac users, copy the disk image file to your hard drive. After it has finished copying, double click it to mount the disk image. Navigate to the mounted disk image and run the installer. After installation the disk image can be unmounted and the DMG can be deleted from the hard drive.
- To install on a network, please see the ReadMe file located on the CD-ROM (navigate to your drive).

To complete the installation of the program you need to open the program and click 'Update' in the pop-up. Please note – this CD-ROM is web-enabled and the content will be downloaded from the internet to your hard drive to populate the CD-ROM with the relevant resources. This only needs to be done on first use; after this you will be able to use the CD-ROM without an internet connection. If at any point any content is updated you will receive another pop-up upon start-up with an internet connection.

What's on the digital component

The digital component contains editable Word documents of resources. There is a simple menu system. Go to the year group that you wish to view and then click on the button for the book, which will launch the relevant overview page. The curriculum links document can also be accessed from the book menu.

Components chart: Years 1–2

	Year 1	Year 2
Autumn Term 1	JASPER'S BEANSTALK	Oliver's Vegetables
Autumn Term 2	OWL BABIES	STICK MAN
Spring Term 1	We're Going on a Bear Hunt	Aliens Love Underpants
Spring Term 2	ZOG	Room on the Broom
Summer Term 1	HANDA'S SURPRISE	The Lighthouse Keeper's Lunch
Summer Term 2	SUPERWORM	Winnie the Witch

Components chart: Years 3–4

	Year 3	Year 4
Autumn Term 1	SCHOLASTIC READ&RESPOND — ANNE FINE: Bill's New Frock	SCHOLASTIC READ&RESPOND — ROALD DAHL: George's Marvellous Medicine
Autumn Term 2	SCHOLASTIC READ&RESPOND — Jill Tomlinson: The Owl Who Was Afraid of the Dark	SCHOLASTIC READ&RESPOND — Michael Morpurgo: Why the Whales Came
Spring Term 1	SCHOLASTIC READ&RESPOND — ROALD DAHL: The Twits	SCHOLASTIC READ&RESPOND — Stig of the Dump
Spring Term 2	SCHOLASTIC READ&RESPOND — Ted Hughes: the Iron Man	SCHOLASTIC READ&RESPOND — Jacqueline Wilson: Hetty Feather
Summer Term 1	SCHOLASTIC READ&RESPOND — Diary of a Wimpy Kid	SCHOLASTIC READ&RESPOND — Millions
Summer Term 2	SCHOLASTIC READ&RESPOND — ROALD DAHL: Danny the Champion of the World	SCHOLASTIC READ&RESPOND — How to Train Your Dragon

Components chart: Years 5–6

	Year 5	Year 6
Autumn Term 1	*Kensuke's Kingdom* – Michael Morpurgo	*Charlotte's Web* – E.B. White
Autumn Term 2	*Charlie and the Chocolate Factory* – Roald Dahl	*One Dog and his Boy* – Eva Ibbotson
Spring Term 1	*Varjak Paw* – SF Said	*Carrie's War* – Nina Bawden
Spring Term 2	*Holes* – Louis Sachar	*The Boy in the Striped Pyjamas* – John Boyne
Summer Term 1	*Amazing Maurice* – Terry Pratchett	*Goodnight Mister Tom* – Michelle Magorian
Summer Term 2	*War Horse* – Michael Morpurgo	*Percy Jackson and the Lightning Thief* – Rick Riordan

Year 1

Autumn Term 1

Jasper's Beanstalk

Page 10

Autumn Term 2

Owl Babies

Page 11

Spring Term 1

We're Going on a
Bear Hunt

Page 12

Spring Term 2

Zog

Page 13

Summer Term 1

Handa's Surprise

Page 14

Summer Term 2

Superworm

Page 15

Curriculum objectives
Pages 16–19

Jasper's Beanstalk:

Overview

Plot

One Monday Jasper finds a bean. Over the course of the week he plants it, waters it, digs, rakes and hoes it, picks off the slugs, mows it, but it does not grow. The next Monday he digs it up again and throws it over his shoulder in despair. While he is not watching, his bean slowly grows and grows. Jasper is delighted and climbs up his beanstalk to look for giants.

About the book

This deceptively simple story – only 96 words long – can provide a wealth of work. The patterned language encourages independent reading and work on the past tense. It links beautifully into any work on fairy tales, days of the week, and growing plants – including growing your own beans. It can lead to discussions around cause and effect, sequencing, patience, disappointment, caring for things and animals.

About the teacher's guide

As well as detailed Guided and Shared reading, *Read & Respond: Jasper's Beanstalk* provides the following activities to cover the English curriculum.

Word reading and spelling
- responding speedily to the correct sound of graphemes
- reading words with 'ed' and 'ly' endings

Comprehension
- developing vocabulary
- making inferences about feelings from Jasper's face
- sequencing the story using clues from time phrases
- retelling the story

Composition
- writing key words
- writing a letter
- planning and writing a story
- writing instructions
- writing and proofreading fascinating facts

Speaking and listening
- creating a performance
- participating in a role play
- exploring ideas by asking 'what if'
- asking relevant questions

Owl Babies:

Overview

Topic links

Animals
Families
Day and night
Woodland

Curriculum links

Science – common animals
Geography – habitats
Art and design – making puppets
Mathematics – materials
Design and technology – using materials
Music – percussive sounds
PSHE

Text types covered

Information
Instructions
Diary
Narrative

By the same author

Can't You Sleep, Little Bear? (Walker Books)

Farmer Duck (Walker Books)

The Pig in the Pond (Walker Books)

Alternative books

The Owl Who Was Afraid of the Dark, by Jill Tomlinson (Egmont)

Where's My Teddy? by Jez Alborough (Walker Books)

Plot

One night, owl babies Sarah, Percy and Bill wake up to find their mother has gone. They hop out of their tree hole to wait for her. Sarah, the oldest, reassures her siblings, encouraging them to huddle up with her on her branch, but even she ends up worrying that their mother is lost. At last their mother returns and all is well.

About the book

This touching story with beautifully atmospheric illustrations will strike a chord with most young children, who will have experienced such feelings of anxiety, caring for or being cared for by siblings, belonging and so on. Despite its length, *Owl Babies* has distinct characterisation between the siblings, a clearly sequenced plot (with opening, build-up, crisis and resolution) and a realistic setting (as the dark crowds around the babies).

About the teacher's guide

As well as detailed Guided and Shared reading, *Read & Respond: Owl Babies* provides the following activities to cover the English curriculum.

Word reading and spelling

- reading and selecting words with common endings
- reading words with contractions
- reading common exception words

Comprehension

- linking to own experiences
- discussing beginning, middle and end
- inferring character from speech
- learning new vocabulary for feelings

Composition

- discussing what they are going to write about
- writing a diary
- writing a similar story and a sequel
- checking for a consistent use of past tense

Speaking and listening

- role play
- discussing ideas for woodland sounds
- discussing food that owls might eat
- evaluating thoughts about the mother owl
- explaining feelings

We're Going on a Bear Hunt:

Overview

◉ Topic links

Families
Adventure
Habitats
Weather

◉ Curriculum links

PE – Bear Hunt relay race
Geography – physical features
Geography – weather
PSHE

◉ Text types covered

Information
Plays
Lists
Narrative

◉ By the same author

Michael Rosen's Sad Book
(Walker Books)

Mustard, Custard, Grumble Belly and Gravy (Bloomsbury)

Little Rabbit Foo Foo (Walker Books)

◉ Alternative books

Bears in the Night, by Stan and Jan Berenstain (HarperCollins Children's Books)

Whatever Next! by Jill Murphy (Macmillan Children's Books)

Plot

A family sets out on a bear hunt (they're not scared!) – through long grass, a river, some mud, a forest, a snowstorm, to the cave where the bear lives. However, when they see the bear they make a very fast retreat home again (back through the cave, the snowstorm, the forest, the mud, the river and the long grass).

About the book

It's almost impossible not to join in with the enthusiasm of the family and the repetitive phrases and made-up words. Glorious onomatopoeic noun phrases and a variety of settings and weather drive the story forward. Helen Oxenbury's beautiful illustrations capture the changing emotions of all – even the poor old bear.

About the teacher's guide

As well as detailed Guided and Shared reading, *Read & Respond: We're Going on a Bear Hunt* provides the following activities to cover the English curriculum.

Word reading and spelling

- blending sounds
- writing sentences from memory
- using the prefix 'un'
- reading and writing words with contractions

Comprehension

- linking the story to own families
- inferring the feelings of the characters
- discussing the book
- enjoying and understanding the story's vocabulary

Composition

- writing sentences
- writing a new version (for example, 'Crocodile hunt')
- editing a story
- writing the bear's version of the story

Speaking and listening

- creating a performance
- asking questions
- group discussion
- articulating opinions

Zog:

Overview

● Topic links

Fairy tales

Dragons

People who help us

● Curriculum links

Art and design – designing a dragon

Mathematics – time

Art and design – making a sculpture

PSHE

● Text types covered

Instructions

Information

Report

Narrative

● By the same author

The Gruffalo (Macmillan Children's Books)

Room on the Broom (Macmillan Children's Books)

Tiddler (Alison Green Books)

Stick Man (Alison Green Books)

Superworm (Alison Green Books)

A Squash and a Squeeze (Alison Green Books)

● Alternative books

George and the Dragon, by Christopher Wormell (Red Fox)

The Paper Bag Princess, by Robert Munsch (Annick Press)

Princess Smartypants, by Babette Cole (Puffin)

Plot

Zog is the keenest and biggest dragon at dragon school, and his dearest wish is to be given one of Madam Dragon's golden stars. But Zog is a hopeless student and each year brings a new disaster. A young princess tends to his wounds, then lets him rescue her to gain his gold star. In due course the princess becomes a doctor and Zog acts as her transport.

About the book

Children will sympathise with Zog's desire for a longed-for golden star and rejoice that he and the princess find their true path. This rhyming tale will inspire all would-be doctors. It might also inspire would-be princesses to think again! It shows the importance of caring for each other and for not sticking to assumed thought patterns about who we are.

About the teacher's guide

As well as detailed Guided and Shared reading, *Read & Respond: Zog* provides the following activities to cover the English curriculum.

Word reading and spelling

- reading and spelling words with contractions
- spelling words with common endings

Comprehension

- sequencing and answering questions about the story
- finding facts and making inferences
- designing their own dragons
- comparing their school with Zog's dragon school
- joining in with phrases from the story
- discussing the meaning of words

Composition

- creating a school poster
- writing instructions for making a papier mâché egg
- writing a new story for the characters
- writing Zog's school report

Speaking and listening

- taking part in a role play
- sharing feelings
- discussing the link between the book and fairy tales
- hot-seating the characters

Handa's Surprise:

Overview

- **Topic links**
  - Africa
  - Food
  - Healthy eating
  - Animals

- **Curriculum links**
  - **Geography** – contrasting non-European country
  - **Geography** – equator
  - **Geography** – weather patterns
  - **Science** – animals

- **Text types covered**
  - Information
  - Narrative
  - Report

- **By the same author**
  - *Handa's Hen* (Walker Books)

- **Alternative books**
  - *Oliver's Vegetables,* by Vivian French (Hodder)
  - *Rosie's Walk,* by Pat Hutchins (Little Simon)
  - *Don't Forget the Bacon!* by Pat Hutchins (Red Fox)

Plot

Handa puts seven fruits in a basket, places the basket on her head and goes to visit her friend Akeyo. But unknown to her, as she walks, different animals steal the fruit from her basket. She is about to arrive with an empty basket when a goat crashes into a tangerine tree. Handa is greatly surprised to remove a basket of tangerines from her head.

About the book

Eight different types of fruit and eight different African animals make up this tale of friendship and surprise. The Kenyan landscape and villages are lovingly realised in the illustrations.

About the teacher's guide

As well as detailed Guided and Shared reading, *Read & Respond: Handa's Surprise* provides the following activities to cover the English curriculum.

Word reading and spelling

- reading and spelling words with contractions
- making plurals
- using the suffixes 'er' and 'est' to compare fruit
- breaking words into syllables

Comprehension

- using expressions to infer Handa and Akeyo's feelings
- using details to infer time passing
- comparing Handa's life to their own
- ordering the story and discussing plot twists

Composition

- writing correctly punctuated sentences about Handa
- writing a narrative for what Handa and Akeyo do next
- creating wanted posters for one of the animals
- writing imaginative sentences describing what Handa feels, sees, hears, tastes and smells

Speaking and listening

- using role play to explore the story
- asking questions and discussing the story in a group
- describing feelings surrounding a kind act
- arguing whether animals know right from wrong
- presenting a weather forecast for Kenya and their home

Superworm:

Overview

● Topic links

Superheroes

Minibeasts

● Curriculum links

Geography – physical and human features

Science – common plants and animals

Design and technology – planning a trap

● Text types covered

Instructions

Narrative

Explanations

Persuasive (advert)

● By the same author

The Gruffalo (Macmillan Children's Books)

Room on the Broom (Macmillan Children's Books)

Tiddler (Alison Green Books)

Stick Man (Alison Green Books)

What the Ladybird Heard (Macmillan Children's Books)

Tyrannosaurus Drip (Macmillan Children's Books)

A Squash and a Squeeze (Alison Green Books)

● Alternative books

Stick Man, by Julia Donaldson (Alison Green Books)

Plot

Superworm is the greatest guy in town: he helps move things, he rescues people, he'll be a swing, a hat – whatever you need. Until one day when he is captured by a crow and enchanted by a Wizard Lizard who forces him to look for treasure. When his friends hear the crow plan to eat Superworm, they mount a rescue: they cover the Wizard Lizard in honey, leaves and a spider's web and drop him in the dump. Superworm is free and back to doing what he does best – everything!

About the book

This humorous story of good versus evil shows the strength of community spirit and teamwork. Axel Scheffler's detailed illustrations capture real-world flora and fauna for this small-time fantasy story. As with *Stick Man*, the reader can see all the different things one stick/worm can be.

About the teacher's guide

As well as detailed Guided and Shared reading, *Read & Respond: Superworm* provides the following activities to cover the English curriculum.

Word reading and spelling

- reading accurately: blending sounds and syllables
- finding words with common endings

Comprehension

- discussing title, events and vocabulary
- using own knowledge to discuss the settings in the book
- using a map to discuss the position of events in the book using accurate language

Composition

- writing dramatic sentences
- creating a super villain
- writing a sequel

Speaking and listening

- discussing in a group how characters could be rescued without using superpowers
- in a group, planning sticky traps for the Wizard Lizard
- creating a performance of the story with finger puppets
- inventing a new superhero

Year 1

Curriculum objectives	Jasper's Beanstalk	Owl Babies	We're Going on a Bear Hunt	Zog	Handa's Surprise	Superworm
Word reading						
To apply phonic knowledge and skills as the route to decode words.	✔	✔				✔
To respond speedily with the correct sound to graphemes for all 40+ phonemes, including, where applicable, alternative sounds for graphemes.	✔	✔	✔	✔		✔
To read accurately by blending the sounds in unfamiliar words containing GPCs that have been taught.			✔	✔		✔
To read common exception words, noting unusual correspondences between spelling and sound and where these occur in the word.		✔				
To read words containing taught GPCs and 's', 'es', 'ing', 'ed', 'er' and 'es' endings.	✔	✔	✔	✔		✔
To read other words of more than one syllable that contain taught GPCs.				✔		✔
To read words with contractions, and understand that the apostrophe represents the omitted letter(s).		✔	✔	✔	✔	✔
To read aloud accurately books that are consistent with their developing phonic knowledge and that do not require them to use other strategies to work out words.						
To re-read these books to build up their fluency and confidence in word reading.						
Comprehension						
To listen to and discuss a wide range of poems, stories and non-fiction at a level beyond that at which they can read independently.						✔
To be encouraged to link what they read or hear read to their own experiences.	✔	✔	✔		✔	✔
To become very familiar with key stories, fairy stories and traditional tales, retelling them and considering their particular characteristics.		✔		✔		✔
To recognise and join in with predictable phrases.		✔	✔	✔		
To appreciate rhymes and poems, and to recite some by heart.						✔
To discuss word meanings, linking new meanings to those already known.	✔	✔	✔	✔		✔

Curriculum objectives	Jasper's Beanstalk	Owl Babies	We're Going on a Bear Hunt	Zog	Handa's Surprise	Superworm
To draw on what they already know or on background information and vocabulary provided by the teacher.		✔	✔	✔		✔
To check that the text makes sense to them as they read and correct inaccurate reading.						✔
To discuss the significance of the title and events.						✔
To make inferences on the basis of what is being said and done.	✔	✔	✔	✔	✔	✔
To predict what might happen on the basis of what has been read so far.						
To participate in discussion about what is read to them, taking turns and listening to what others say.	✔	✔	✔	✔	✔	✔
To explain clearly their understanding of what is read to them.	✔	✔	✔	✔	✔	✔
Transcription: Spelling						
To spell words containing each of the 40+ phonemes already taught.	✔		✔			
To learn to spell common exception words.				✔		
To learn to spell the days of the week.		✔				✔
To name the letters of the alphabet in order.		✔			✔	
To use letter names to distinguish between alternative spellings of the same sound.						
To use the spelling rule for adding 's' or 'es' as the plural marker for nouns and the third person singular marker for verbs.					✔	
To use the prefix 'un'.			✔			
To use 'ing', 'ed', 'er' and 'est' where no change is needed in the spelling of root words.			✔	✔	✔	✔
To apply simple spelling rules and guidance, as listed in English Appendix 1.	✔	✔	✔	✔	✔	✔
To write from memory simple sentences dictated by the teacher that include words using the GPCs and common exception words taught so far.			✔	✔		✔

Year 1

Curriculum objectives	Jasper's Beanstalk	Owl Babies	We're Going on a Bear Hunt	Zog	Handa's Surprise	Superworm
Handwriting						
To sit correctly at a table, holding a pencil comfortably and correctly.						
To begin to form lower-case letters in the correct direction, starting and finishing in the right place.	✓	✓				
To form capital letters.						
To form digits 0–9.						
To understand which letters belong to which handwriting 'families' and to practise these.						
Composition						
To say out loud what they are going to write about.	✓	✓	✓	✓	✓	
To compose a sentence orally before writing it.						✓
To sequence sentences to form short narratives.		✓	✓	✓	✓	
To re-read what they have written to check that it makes sense.	✓	✓		✓		
To discuss what they have written with the teacher or other pupils.		✓	✓	✓		✓
To read aloud what they have written clearly enough to be heard by their peers and the teacher.		✓		✓		
Composition: Grammar, vocabulary and punctuation						
To leave spaces between words.					✓	
To join words and sentences using 'and'.					✓	
To begin to punctuate sentences using a capital letter and a full stop, question mark or exclamation mark.		✓	✓	✓	✓	✓
To use a capital letter for names of people, places, the days of the week, and the personal pronoun 'I'.				✓		
To learn the grammar for Year 1 in English Appendix 2.	✓	✓	✓	✓	✓	✓
To use the grammatical terminology in English Appendix 2 in discussing their writing.		✓				

Year 1

Curriculum objectives	Jasper's Beanstalk	Owl Babies	We're Going on a Bear Hunt	Zog	Handa's Surprise	Superworm
Spoken language						
To listen and respond appropriately to adults and their peers.						
To ask relevant questions to extend their understanding and knowledge.	✓					
To use relevant strategies to build their vocabulary.						
To articulate and justify answers, arguments and opinions.				✓	✓	
To give well-structured descriptions, explanations and narratives for different purposes, including for expressing feelings.	✓	✓			✓	
To maintain attention and participate actively in collaborative conversations, staying on topic and initiating and responding to comments.	✓	✓		✓	✓	
To use spoken language to develop understanding through speculating, hypothesising, imagining and exploring ideas.	✓					
To speak audibly and fluently with an increasing command of Standard English.						
To participate in discussions, presentations, performances, role play, improvisations and debates.	✓	✓		✓	✓	
To gain, maintain and monitor the interest of the listeners.						
To consider and evaluate different viewpoints, attending to and building on the contributions of others.		✓				
To select and use appropriate registers for effective communication.						

Year 2

Autumn Term 1

Oliver's Vegetables

Page 21

Autumn Term 2

Stick Man

Page 22

Spring Term 1

Aliens Love
Underpants

Page 23

Spring Term 2

Room on the Broom

Page 24

Summer Term 1

The Lighthouse
Keeper's Lunch

Page 25

Summer Term 2

Winnie the Witch

Page 26

Curriculum objectives
Pages 27–30

Oliver's Vegetables:

Overview

Topic links

Healthy eating

Science

Food

Staying away from home

Curriculum links

Science – common plants

Science – healthy eating

Design and technology – nutrition and cooking

Art – illustrating

PSHE

Text types covered

Explanation

Narrative

Persuasive

Instructions

Information

By the same author

Oliver's Fruit Salad (Hodder Children's Books)

Oliver's Milkshake (Hodder Children's Books)

Yucky Worms (Walker Books)

Alternative books

Jasper's Beanstalk, by Nick Butterworth (Hodder Children's Books)

I Will Not Ever Never Eat a Tomato, by Lauren Child (Orchard Books)

Plot

Oliver only eats chips but when he goes to stay with his grandparents for a week, he strikes up a deal with his grandfather: if he can find the potatoes in his grandfather's garden, he can have chips; but if he finds any other vegetables he has to eat those without grumbling. Throughout the week, Oliver finds, eats and enjoys: carrots, spinach, rhubarb, cabbage, beetroot and peas.

About the book

Oliver's Vegetables fits in perfectly with any unit on healthy eating, and fun can be had trying and growing any of the vegetables in the book. It can also be used to discuss how things grow, grandparents, staying away from home, being brave, trying things, days of the week, colours and a healthy lifestyle. It lends itself to small-world play and work can be extended using the sequels *Oliver's Fruit Salad* and *Oliver's Milkshake* (both Hodder Children's Books).

About the teacher's guide

As well as detailed Guided and Shared reading, *Read & Respond: Oliver's Vegetables* provides the following activities to cover the English curriculum.

Word reading and spelling
- reading words with common endings
- reading and spelling common exception words
- reading and understanding new vocabulary

Comprehension
- matching days of the week to vegetables found and eaten
- comparing Oliver's diet to their own
- using the text to draw Grandpa's vegetable patch

Composition
- creating a healthy eating poster
- writing a poem inspired by a vegetable tasting session
- researching and writing a set of instructions for growing peas
- investigating minibeasts and writing a set of labels

Speaking and listening
- talking about staying away from home
- planning a menu as a group
- participating in a debate about slugs
- presenting facts about healthy eating

Stick Man:

Overview

◉ Topic links

Countryside
Woodland
Christmas
Seasons

◉ Curriculum links

Art – making a stick man
Science – common plants and animals
Geography – seasons
Geography – human and physical features

◉ Text types covered

Instructions
Poetry
Narrative
Information
Report

◉ By the same author

The Gruffalo (Macmillan Children's Books)

Room on the Broom (Macmillan Children's Books)

Tiddler (Alison Green Books)

Zog (Alison Green Books)

A Squash and a Squeeze (Alison Green Books)

◉ Alternative books

Unfortunately, by Alan Durant (Orchard Books)

Tiddler, by Julia Donaldson (Alison Green Books)

Plot

When Stick Man goes for a jog one spring morning, he gets taken miles from his home as a range of different people and animals mistake him for a useful stick. As he travels through the British countryside, the seasons change and different animals and activities can be seen in the background. Months later and miles from home he hears Santa stuck in a chimney. He rescues Santa, who in turn takes him home to his family.

About the book

The easy rhythm and rhyme of the story makes *Stick Man* ideal for reading aloud with the children joining in, as well as retelling and writing their own versions. Discussions can centre on prediction, cause and effect, what the children do as the seasons change and Christmas traditions.

About the teacher's guide

As well as detailed Guided and Shared reading, *Read & Respond: Stick Man* provides the following activities to cover the English curriculum.

Word reading and spelling

- spelling words containing the /k/ sound
- adding the suffixes 'ing', 'ed', 's', 'ly' and 'ful'
- reading and spelling words with contractions
- using 'when', 'because', 'but', 'that'
- spelling homophones and the days of the week

Comprehension

- sequencing events, showing cause and effect
- making inferences about the characters and time
- plotting the story against the seasons and countryside
- spotting plants and animals that create setting

Composition

- creating a poster to advertise a park
- writing a similar story and a sequel
- composing a rhyming chorus for a fairy-tale character
- writing a set of instructions for making a pine-cone fairy

Speaking and listening

- performing a version of the story
- learning a song version
- arguing for or against given statements about the book
- giving a presentation about the seasons

Aliens Love Underpants:

Overview

◉ Topic links

Space

◉ Curriculum links

Art – space themed

Design and technology – model spaceships

Science – different materials

Mathematics – patterns

PE – creating a games day

PSHE

◉ Text types covered

Instructions

Poetry

Report

Narrative

Letter

Book review

◉ By the same author

Monster Max's Shark Spaghetti (Bloomsbury Children's)

Monsters Love Underpants (Simon & Schuster)

Superkid (Scholastic)

Spider Sandwiches (Bloomsbury)

◉ Alternative books

Pants, by Giles Andreae (Corgi)

Beegu, by Alexis Deacon (Red Fox)

Man on the Moon, by Simon Bartram (Templar Publishing)

Plot

Aliens love underpants: they love everything about them, including their colours, patterns and shapes. Sadly, there are no underpants on the planet where they live and so they zoom towards Earth in their spaceship in search of them. In a flash, they land and rush around collecting underpants. But … as soon as Mum appears to bring in the washing, the aliens vanish as quickly as they appeared.

About the book

This book provides children with delightful opportunities to have fun and enjoy talking, reading and writing about a subject they think is a bit 'naughty'. The rhyming couplet pattern of the text will help to develop children's ability to appreciate and experiment with the effects of carefully chosen words and rhyme. The book also provides an opportunity to enter the crazy world of a bunch of quirky aliens, where anything goes!

About the teacher's guide

As well as detailed Guided and Shared reading, *Read & Respond: Aliens Love Underpants* provides the following activities to cover the English curriculum.

Word reading and spelling

- reading words with known phonemes
- adding the suffixes 'ing', 'ed', 'er', 'est', 's', 'es'
- reading words with contractions

Comprehension

- linking to own experience
- exploring settings (different planets)
- describing aliens
- inferring characters' feelings
- sequencing the story
- reciting poetry

Composition

- writing a book review
- writing a letter to an alien
- creating a photographic diary
- writing a sequel
- writing a recipe for an edible alien

Speaking and listening

- role-playing different endings

Room on the Broom:

Overview

● Topic links

Friendship

Weather

Halloween

Fairy tale

● Curriculum links

Art and design – model making

Design and technology – designing a flying machine

Music – using percussion

Science – weight

PSHE

● Text types covered

Instructions

Poetry

Information

Narrative

Poster

● By the same author

The Gruffalo (Macmillan Children's Books)

Stick Man (Macmillan Children's Books)

Tiddler (Alison Green Books)

Zog (Alison Green Books)

A Squash and a Squeeze (Alison Green Books)

● Alternative books

The Smartest Giant in Town, by Julia Donaldson (Macmillan Children's Books)

A Squash and a Squeeze, by Julia Donaldson (Macmillan Children's Books)

Plot

One day, as a witch and her cat are flying on her broom, the wind blows off the witch's hat. When she retrieves it, a dog asks to join her on the broom and she agrees. Soon she loses her bow, gains a bird; loses her wand and gains a frog. When the broom snaps in two with the weight of her the animals they end up in a bog and the witch is caught by a dragon. Her muddy friends shout at the dragon: they look like a mud monster to him and he flies away. The witch creates a new improved broom with plenty of room for all her friends.

About the book

The characters in this story might be from a fairy tale but they demonstrate the importance of friendship, kindness and teamwork. Wind, rain, mud, light and dark do not deter their happy spirit. The strong rhythm and rhyme will encourage participation. The broom itself can be used to discuss weights and balances.

About the teacher's guide

As well as detailed Guided and Shared reading, *Read & Respond: Room on the Broom* provides the following activities to cover the English curriculum.

Word reading and spelling

- spelling words with common endings
- practising known spellings for phonemes
- writing simple dictated sentences
- comparing the spelling of rhyming words

Comprehension

- sequencing events
- making inferences
- describing settings
- joining in with predictable phrases

Composition

- writing a poem inspired by the story
- composing a magical spell
- creating a witch and writing a descriptive passage
- designing a flying machine

Speaking and listening

- hot-seating the characters
- role-playing new scenes
- articulating opinions on alternative endings

The Lighthouse Keeper's Lunch:
Overview

Topic links
Seaside
Holidays
Food

Curriculum links
Geography – key features
History – how life has changed
Science – animals, the seasons
Design and technology – designing and evaluating

Text types covered
Information
Poetry
Playscript
Diary
Narrative
Instructions
Report

By the same author
The Lighthouse Keeper's New Friend (Scholastic)

The Lighthouse Keeper's Breakfast (Scholastic)

The Lighthouse Keeper's Picnic (Scholastic)

Small Knight and George (Orchard Books)

Alternative books
The Mousehole Cat, by Antonia Barber (Walker Books)

Winnie at the Seaside, by Valerie Thomas (Oxford University Press)

Plot
Every morning, come rain or shine, Mr Grinling travels out to his lighthouse. Every day, Mrs Grinling makes Mr Grinling a tasty picnic lunch and sends it across to him on a wire. One day, however, a group of seagulls discovers the flying lunch and eat the lot. Mrs Grinling tries to protect the picnic. In the end, she fills the sandwiches with mustard and the seagulls leave to find their lunch elsewhere.

About the book
The Lighthouse Keeper's Lunch has a clearly sequenced plot, distinct characters and setting. The children will need help with the glorious vocabulary but soon they will enjoy a level of poetic writing not usually found in picture books.

About the teacher's guide
As well as detailed Guided and Shared reading, *Read & Respond: The Lighthouse Keeper's Lunch* provides the following activities to cover the English curriculum.

Word reading and spelling
- sorting graphemes into different sounds
- practising spelling common exception words
- reading and spelling words with contractions
- joining clauses with 'and' or 'but'
- spelling the days of the week

Comprehension
- discussing the complex vocabulary
- making inferences about the characters
- sequencing the events of the plot

Composition
- writing Mrs Grinling's diary
- writing a new adventure for Mr Grinling
- composing a seaside poem
- describing a personal trip to the seaside
- writing a recipe for a lighthouse sandwich

Speaking and listening
- presenting a television news report
- reciting a related poem
- creating a performance of the book
- interviewing Mr Grinling
- discussing the benefit of different ways to protect the lunch

Winnie the Witch:

Overview

Topic links

Colours

Halloween

Problem solving

Pets

Curriculum links

Art – appreciating illustrations

Science – animals

Computing – problem solving

PSHE

Text types covered

Information

Narrative

Poetry

Advert

Letter

By the same author

Winnie at the Seaside (Oxford University Press)

Winnie's Midnight Dragon (Oxford University Press)

Winnie's Magic Wand (Oxford University Press)

Winnie's Amazing Pumpkin (Oxford University Press)

Alternative books

Meg and Mog, by Helen Nicoll (Puffin)

The Worst Witch, by Jill Murphy (Puffin)

Elmer, by David McKee (Andersen Press)

Plot

Everything in Winnie the Witch's house is black: the stairs, the chairs, the bath and her long-suffering cat Wilbur. When Wilbur is awake, Winnie can only see his green eyes; when Wilbur is asleep, Winnie cannot see him at all and sits on him or trips over him. Turning Wilbur green seems to work well, until Winnie trips over him in the grass. Winnie tries turning Wilbur multi-coloured, but the birds laugh at him. In the end she finds the perfect solution: Wilbur stays black but she turns the house and all its contents different colours.

About the book

The gentle humour coupled with Korky Paul's comic illustrations makes this an excellent story. Repetitive language creates a model to imitate and the endearing characters can be discussed and reused. Further details for plot, character, setting and atmosphere can all be inferred from the marvellous illustrations.

About the teacher's guide

As well as detailed Guided and Shared reading, *Read & Respond: Winnie the Witch* provides the following activities to cover the English curriculum.

Word reading and spelling

- reading and spelling words with contractions
- creating plurals and comparisons
- breaking a word into syllables

Comprehension

- predicting events and discussing cause and effect
- comparing their house with Winnie's house
- creating dialogue for the story
- discussing the sequence of events

Composition

- writing a sequel
- creating an advert for animal adoption
- creating longer sentences about cats
- writing a letter to Valerie Thomas or Korky Paul
- writing their own spell

Speaking and listening

- hot-seating the characters
- creating new magic words
- role playing a scene between Wilbur and the birds
- interpreting Winnie and Wilbur's facial expressions
- justifying opinions about Winnie's behaviour

Curriculum objectives	Oliver's Vegetables	Stick Man	Aliens Love Underpants	Room on the Broom	Lighthouse Keeper's Lunch	Winnie the Witch
Word reading						
To continue to apply phonic knowledge and skills as the route to decode words until automatic decoding has become embedded and reading is fluent.			✔	✔	✔	✔
To read accurately by blending the sounds in words that contain the graphemes taught so far, especially recognising alternative sounds for graphemes.	✔		✔	✔	✔	
To read accurately words of two or more syllables that contain the same graphemes as above.	✔			✔		
To read words containing common suffixes.	✔				✔	
To read further common exception words, noting unusual correspondences between spelling and sound and where these occur in the word.	✔					
To read most words quickly and accurately, without overt sounding and blending, when they have been frequently encountered.						
To read aloud books closely matched to their improving phonic knowledge, sounding out unfamiliar words accurately, automatically and without undue hesitation.						
To re-read these books to build up their fluency and confidence in word reading.						
Comprehension						
To listen to, discuss and express views about a wide range of contemporary and classic poetry, stories and non-fiction at a level beyond that at which they can read independently.		✔	✔	✔		✔
To discuss the sequence of events in books and how items of information are related.	✔	✔		✔	✔	✔
To become increasingly familiar with and retell a wider range of stories, fairy stories and traditional tales.		✔	✔	✔		
To be introduced to non-fiction books that are structured in different ways.	✔	✔	✔	✔	✔	
To recognise simple recurring literary language in stories and poetry.		✔	✔	✔		
To discuss and clarify the meanings of words, linking new meanings to known vocabulary.	✔	✔			✔	
To discuss their favourite words and phrases.						
To continue to build up a repertoire of poems learned by heart, appreciating these and reciting some, with appropriate intonation to make the meaning clear.			✔		✔	
To draw on what they already know or on background information and vocabulary provided by the teacher.	✔	✔	✔	✔	✔	✔
To check that the text makes sense to them as they read and correct inaccurate reading.						
To make inferences on the basis of what is being said and done.	✔	✔	✔	✔	✔	✔
To answer and ask questions.						

Year 2

Curriculum objectives	Oliver's Vegetables	Stick Man	Aliens Love Underpants	Room on the Broom	Lighthouse Keeper's Lunch	Winnie the Witch
To predict what might happen on the basis of what has been read so far.	✔	✔	✔	✔		✔
To participate in discussion about books, poems and other works that are read to them and those that they can read for themselves, taking turns and listening to what others say.		✔	✔	✔	✔	✔
To explain and discuss their understanding of books, poems and other material, both those that they listen to and those that they read for themselves.	✔		✔	✔		
Transcription: Spelling						
To segment spoken words into phonemes and represent these by graphemes, spelling many correctly.		✔	✔			
To learn new ways of spelling phonemes for which one or more spellings are already known, and learn some words with each spelling, including a few common homophones.		✔				
To learn to spell common exception words.					✔	
To learn to spell more words with contracted forms.		✔	✔		✔	
To learn the possessive apostrophe (singular) (for example, the girl's book).						
To distinguish between homophones and near-homophones.						
To add suffixes to spell longer words, including 'ment', 'ness', 'ful', 'less', 'ly'.			✔			
To apply spelling rules and guidance, as listed in English Appendix 1.	✔	✔	✔	✔	✔	✔
To write from memory simple sentences dictated by the teacher that include words using the GPCs, common exception words and punctuation taught so far.			✔	✔		
Handwriting						
To form lower-case letters of the correct size relative to one another.						
To start using some of the diagonal and horizontal strokes needed to join letters and understand which letters, when adjacent to one another, are best left unjoined.						
To write capital letters and digits of the correct size, orientation and relationship to one another and to lower case letters.						
To use spacing between words that reflects the size of the letters.						

Year 2

Curriculum objectives	Oliver's Vegetables	Stick Man	Aliens Love Underpants	Room on the Broom	Lighthouse Keeper's Lunch	Winnie the Witch
Composition						
To write narratives about personal experiences and those of others (real and fictional).	✓	✓	✓	✓	✓	
To write about real events.						
To write poetry.	✓	✓		✓	✓	
To write for different purposes.	✓	✓	✓	✓	✓	
To plan or say out loud what they are going to write about.		✓	✓	✓	✓	✓
To write down ideas and/or key words, including new vocabulary.		✓			✓	
To encapsulate what they want to say, sentence by sentence.	✓					
To evaluate their writing with the teacher and other children.			✓	✓		
To re-read to check that their writing makes sense and that verbs to indicate time are used correctly and consistently, including verbs in the continuous form.		✓				
To proofread to check for errors in spelling, grammar and punctuation (for example, ends of sentences punctuated correctly).			✓		✓	
To read aloud what they have written with appropriate intonation to make the meaning clear.			✓	✓		
Composition: Grammar, vocabulary and punctuation						
To learn how to use both familiar and new punctuation correctly (see English Appendix 2), including full stops, capital letters, exclamation marks, question marks, commas for lists and apostrophes for contracted forms and the possessive (singular).		✓		✓		✓
To write sentences with different forms: statement, question, exclamation, command.		✓				
To use expanded noun phrases to describe and specify (for example, 'the blue butterfly').	✓	✓			✓	✓
To use the present and past tenses correctly and consistently including the progressive form.					✓	✓

Year 2

Curriculum objectives	Oliver's Vegetables	Stick Man	Aliens Love Underpants	Room on the Broom	Lighthouse Keeper's Lunch	Winnie the Witch
To use subordination (using 'when', 'if', 'that' or 'because') and coordination (using 'or', 'and' or 'but').		✓			✓	✓
To use the grammar for Year 2 in English Appendix 2.	✓	✓	✓	✓	✓	✓
To use some features of written Standard English.						
To use and understand the grammatical terminology in English Appendix 2 in discussing their writing.						
Spoken language						
To listen and respond appropriately to adults and their peers.						✓
To ask relevant questions to extend their understanding and knowledge.	✓				✓	
To use relevant strategies to build their vocabulary.						✓
To articulate and justify answers, arguments and opinions.	✓	✓				✓
To give well-structured descriptions, explanations and narratives for different purposes, including for expressing feelings.	✓	✓			✓	✓
To maintain attention and participate actively in collaborative conversations, staying on topic and initiating and responding to comments.	✓	✓				✓
To use spoken language to develop understanding through speculating, hypothesising, imagining and exploring ideas.					✓	
To speak audibly and fluently with an increasing command of Standard English.						
To participate in discussions, presentations, performances, role play, improvisations and debates.	✓	✓			✓	✓
To gain, maintain and monitor the interest of the listeners.						
To consider and evaluate different viewpoints, attending to and building on the contributions of others.		✓			✓	
To select and use appropriate registers for effective communication.						

Year 3

Autumn Term 1

Bill's New Frock

Page 32

Autumn Term 2

The Owl Who Was
Afraid of the Dark

Page 33

Spring Term 1

The Twits

Page 34

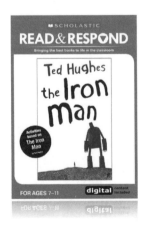

Spring Term 2

The Iron Man

Page 35

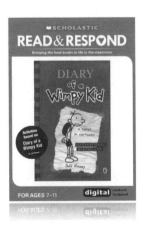

Summer Term 1

Diary of a Wimpy Kid

Page 36

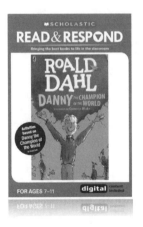

Summer Term 2

Danny the Champion
of the World

Page 37

Curriculum objectives
Pages 38–41

Bill's New Frock:

Overview

● Topic links

Jobs people do

School

Gender

How we dress

● Curriculum links

PE – Paralympics

Geography – weather

Art – comic strip

PSHE

● Text types covered

Information

Playscripts

Poetry

Narrative

Comic strip

● By the same author

The Diary of a Killer Cat (Puffin)

Flour Babies (Puffin)

Goggle-eyes (Puffin)

The Angel of Nitshill Road (Egmont)

Madame Doubtfire (Puffin)

● Alternative books

Princess Smartypants, by Babette Cole (Puffin)

The Diary of a Killer Cat, by Anne Fine (Puffin)

Plot

One day Bill wakes up to find out that he has changed into a girl. Before he can say anything, he is given a frilly dress to wear and sent off to school. At school, everyone treats him differently: the bully, his classmates and the school staff. People use different language when talking to him and have different expectations of him. And as the day goes on, Bill's dress gets dirtier and dirtier.

About the book

Based on Anne Fine's own experiences, *Bill's New Frock* humorously confronts the very serious subject of gender stereotyping at an appropriate level for this age group.

About the teacher's guide

As well as detailed Guided and Shared reading, *Read & Respond: Bill's New Frock* provides the following activities to cover the English curriculum.

Word reading and spelling

- understanding word families
- using 'a' or 'an'
- spelling words with the /shun/ phoneme and using the suffix 'ous'

Comprehension

- discussing main ideas in a paragraph
- drawing inferences
- identifying and discussing the theme of gender inequality

Composition

- planning paragraphs
- using and punctuating direct speech
- note taking
- using weather to write paragraphs about feelings
- writing a new version of the poem 'Sugar and spice'
- writing new scenes for the book
- creating a non-fiction text about gender

Speaking and listening

- evaluating different viewpoints about clothes
- debating girl footballers, female ballet dancers and whether there should be some jobs only done by men or women
- creating an improvisation around Bill's parents
- asking questions: hot-seating Bill

The Owl Who Was Afraid of the Dark:
Overview

● Topic links

Night and day
Woodland life
Festivals

● Curriculum links

Science – common animals
Geography – British locations
Geography – maps
Art – appreciating art
Art – trying techniques
PSHE

● Text types covered

Information
Interview
Mind maps
Narrative
Presentation
Persuasive
Poetry

● By the same author

The Penguin Who Wanted to Find Out (Egmont)

The Otter Who Wanted to Know (Egmont)

The Hen Who Wouldn't Give Up (Egmont)

The Cat Who Wanted to Go Home (Egmont)

● Alternative books

Owl Babies, by Martin Waddell (Walker Books)

The Owl Who Was Afraid of the Dark, abridged picture book version (Walker Books)

Plot

Plop, a fat, fluffy baby barn owl, is frightened of the dark. His frustrated mother tells him to find out about it to overcome his fear. Over a few days he meets and talks to a number of people who tell him why they love the dark. Eventually he goes on a night walk with a cat who shows him how beautiful the night is and he realises, at last, that he is a night bird.

About the book

The Owl Who Was Afraid of the Dark is a tale of how we can overcome our fears by asking questions, and about identity. Although the book is a gentle fantasy, the setting is carefully based in fact as we learn about how barn owls care for their young: where they sleep and how and what they feed them. Set the week after bonfire night, this is a great autumn story.

About the teacher's guide

As well as detailed Guided and Shared reading, *Read & Respond: The Owl Who Was Afraid of the Dark* provides the following activities to cover the English curriculum.

Word reading and spelling
- adding prefixes and suffixes correctly
- practising commonly misspelled words

Comprehension
- identifying how a baby owl changes and grows
- asking questions about barn owls and investigating nocturnal animals
- inferring and describing feelings
- listening to woodland sounds

Composition
- using conjunctions to show cause and effect
- using fronted adverbials, speech marks, apostrophes
- writing a night-time or owl poem
- writing a new chapter
- creating a leaflet advertising a night-time walk

Speaking and listening
- participating in a role play of one chapter
- giving a presentation about barn owls in danger
- debating whether dark is exciting or not
- practising listening to and referring to others' ideas

The Twits:

Overview

- ◉ **Topic links**

  Roald Dahl

  Funny stories

- ◉ **Curriculum links**

  PSHE

  Citizenship

  Science – animals

- ◉ **Text types covered**

  Information

  Advert

  Narrative

  Instructions

  Presentations

  Drama

  Poetry

  News report

- ◉ **By the same author**

  The BFG (Puffin)

  Danny the Champion of the World (Puffin)

  Charlie and the Chocolate Factory (Puffin)

  Matilda (Puffin)

  George's Marvellous Medicine (Puffin)

  The Enormous Crocodile (Puffin)

- ◉ **Alternative books**

  The Enormous Crocodile, by Roald Dahl (Puffin)

  You're a Bad Man, Mr Gum! by Andy Stanton (Egmont)

Plot

Mr and Mrs Twit are the meanest and most revolting couple you could ever meet. They play foul and cruel tricks on each other and they torment a group of circus monkeys they keep in their garden. Eventually the monkeys, with a Roly-Poly Bird from Africa, play a last devious trick on the horrid pair – and Mr and Mrs Twit are no more.

About the book

As you would expect from Roald Dahl, *The Twits* is filled with foul humour, glorious new words, bizarre events and strange and revolting characters.

About the teacher's guide

As well as detailed Guided and Shared reading, *Read & Respond: The Twits* provides the following activities to cover the English curriculum.

Word reading and spelling

- using prefixes to change meaning, creating descriptions
- adding the suffix 'ly' to change adjectives
- exploring word families

Comprehension

- creating a character profile and 'wanted poster'
- discussing the intricacies of the plot

Composition

- changing the plot
- creating dialogue and punctuating speech
- using possessive apostrophes and fronted adverbials
- writing an advert
- making up a new stanza for the Roly-Poly Bird's rhyme
- researching and writing a monkey fact file
- writing a fairy-tale version of the book, adding magic

Speaking and listening

- creating a spoken advert for a made-up glue
- creating tableaux, mimes and role plays for different scenes
- discussing a variety of conventional story stereotypes
- interviewing the characters to get different points of view
- justifying an opinion that beards are great

The Iron Man:

Overview

Topic links

Space

Robots

Curriculum links

Art and design

PSHE

RE

Geography – countries

Science – forces, magnets

Text types covered

Diary

Explanation

Playscript

Newspaper report

Book review

Narrative

By the same author

The Iron Woman (Faber & Faber)

How the Whale Became and Other Stories (Faber & Faber)

Alternative books

The Selfish Giant, by Oscar Wilde (Puffin)

'The Lion and the Mouse', by Aesop

Wendel's Workshop, by Chris Riddell (Macmillan)

Plot

A mysterious iron giant topples over a cliff edge and breaks into pieces. The pieces reassemble themselves and the Iron Man goes on a hungry rampage, devouring farm machinery and fencing, causing the farmers to rise up in a warlike response. A farmer's young son, Hogarth, finds a solution. When a monster from outer space attacks the planet, it is the Iron Man's turn to negotiate.

About the book

The Iron Man is a form of fairy tale or allegory. Generic characters inhabit the story, making the characters seem very distant apart from a huge robot and a small boy. Together they teach the reader compromise and the pointlessness of fighting.

About the teacher's guide

As well as detailed Guided and Shared reading, *Read & Respond: The Iron Man* provides the following activities to cover the English curriculum.

Word reading and spelling

• spelling homophones

Comprehension

• finding main ideas and making notes across the story
• creating descriptive versions of the setting
• inferring the feelings of the characters and discussing their own responses
• analysing the passing of time in the story
• comparing the opening with *The Iron Woman*

Composition

• using clauses and fronted adverbials
• using nouns and pronouns correctly
• punctuating direct speech
• preparing notes for a film version
• writing a playscript for part of the text
• creating a newspaper report

Speaking and listening

• presenting a news bulletin about the events
• discussing the nature of the space-bat-angel-dragon
• debating why people go to war
• comparing the book with a film version and sequel

Diary of a Wimpy Kid:

Overview

⦿ Topic links

Cartoons
Books and films
School stories
How we change
Families

⦿ Curriculum links

PSHE
Geography – countries
RE – festivals

⦿ Text types covered

Persuasive
Narrative
Diary
Information
Interview
Leaflet
Letters

⦿ By the same author

Diary of a Wimpy Kid: Rodrick Rules
(Puffin)

Diary of a Wimpy Kid: The Last Straw
(Puffin)

Diary of a Wimpy Kid: Dog Days
(Puffin)

Diary of a Wimpy Kid: The Ugly Truth
(Puffin)

⦿ Alternative books

Bill's New Frock, by Anne Fine
(Egmont)

Captain Underpants, by Dav Pilkey
(Scholastic)

Plot

A (school) year in the life of middle-schooler Greg Heffley, whose diary entries describe his plans for glory and his actual failures. Poor Greg is filled with great ideas, but nothing seems to go right for him: not the school play, snowman-building, the comic-strip competition, and certainly not his relationship with his friends and family. But he's not going to let that get him down!

About the book

It's not easy being a weedy kid who is desperate to be one of the cool kids. We can all identify with Greg's mistakes and longings. We can laugh with him – and at him – but we also learn about the dangers of lies, and not seeing what is truly important in life. *Diary of a Wimpy Kid* is a great book for talking about the trials of peer pressure, but also using different formats, creating a 'voice' and using the first person.

About the teacher's guide

As well as detailed Guided and Shared reading, *Read & Respond: Diary of a Wimpy Kid* provides the following activities to cover the English curriculum.

Word reading and spelling
• using a range of suffixes and prefixes

Comprehension
• analysing how the combination of text, speech and cartoons adds to meaning
• inferring the motivations and feelings of characters

Composition
• using inverted commas and apostrophes
• using conjunctions, adverbs (included fronted) and prepositions to explain time, place and cause
• writing letters
• creating a cartoon of an amusing incident
• writing year book entries

Speaking and listening
• discussing what makes people popular – and whether these are good judgements to have
• discussing embarrassing scenarios
• discussing what makes a good friend
• considering different views of Halloween

Danny the Champion of the World:
Overview

● Topic links

Countryside
Roald Dahl
Families
Bullies

● Curriculum links

PSHE
Science – animals
History – local history study
Design and technology – design and evaluate

● Text types covered

Narrative
Information
Letter
Instructions
Book review

● By the same author

The BFG (Puffin)
Charlie and the Chocolate Factory (Puffin)
Matilda (Puffin)
George's Marvellous Medicine (Puffin)
The Enormous Crocodile (Puffin)

● Alternative books

The Enormous Crocodile, by Roald Dahl (Puffin)
George's Marvellous Medicine, by Roald Dahl (Puffin)

Plot

Danny and his father live in a gypsy caravan behind a petrol station where Danny's father is a car mechanic. When Danny discovers that his father is a poacher on the side, he works with him to devise a plan to ruin the annual pheasant shoot of evil local land owner Mr Victor Hazell. Together they scatter the woods with raisins laced with sleeping powder and return later to collect 200 sleeping pheasants. Although the vicar's wife hides the pheasants, they start to wake up, cause mayhem and fly away. But the shooting party is still ruined and everyone agrees that Danny is the world's greatest poacher.

About the book

The story of *Danny the Champion of the World* is about good versus evil, community spirit and the loving relationship between father and son. Like other favourite Dahl stories, the plot turns on evil bullies being stopped by cunning plans and clever tricks.

About the teacher's guide

As well as detailed Guided and Shared reading, *Read & Respond: Danny the Champion of the World* provides the following activities to cover the English curriculum.

Word reading and spelling
- spelling a range of homophones

Comprehension
- inferring details about the relationship between Danny and his father
- comparing a variety of Dahl villains
- describing the woodland setting and 1970s setting

Composition
- extending sentences using clauses
- using pronouns and fronted adverbials to create flow
- creating a storyboard for a film version
- writing a set of instructions for making a toy
- writing a letter in character

Speaking and listening
- comparing their lives with Danny's
- participating in a debate about shooting pheasants
- participating in a performance of part of the story
- exploring the issue of a child driving a vehicle

Year 3

Curriculum objectives	Bill's New Frock	The Owl Who Was Afraid of the Dark	The Twits	The Iron Man	Diary of a Wimpy Kid	Danny the Champion of the World
Word reading						
To apply their growing knowledge of root words, prefixes and suffixes (etymology and morphology) as listed in English Appendix 1, both to read aloud and to understand the meaning of new words they meet.	✔	✔	✔	✔	✔	✔
To read further exception words, noting the unusual correspondences between spelling and sound, and where these occur in the word.						
Comprehension						
To develop positive attitudes to reading and an understanding of what they read.	✔	✔	✔	✔	✔	✔
To listen to and discuss a wide range of fiction, poetry, plays, non-fiction and reference books or textbooks.						
To read books that are structured in different ways and read for a range of purposes.		✔		✔		✔
To use dictionaries to check the meaning of words that they have read.						
To increase their familiarity with a wide range of books, including fairy stories, myths and legends, and retell some of these orally.		✔				
To identify themes and conventions in a wide range of books.	✔	✔	✔	✔	✔	✔
To prepare poems and playscripts to read aloud and to perform, showing understanding through intonation, tone, volume and action.				✔		
To discuss words and phrases that capture the reader's interest and imagination.		✔	✔	✔		✔
To recognise some different forms of poetry (for example, free verse, narrative poetry).						
To check that the text makes sense to them, discussing their understanding and explaining the meaning of words in context.			✔	✔	✔	
To ask questions to improve their understanding of a text.		✔	✔		✔	
To draw inferences such as inferring characters' feelings, thoughts and motives from their actions, and justify inferences with evidence.	✔	✔	✔	✔	✔	✔
To predict what might happen from details stated and implied.					✔	

Year 3

Curriculum objectives	Bill's New Frock	The Owl Who Was Afraid of the Dark	The Twits	The Iron Man	Diary of a Wimpy Kid	Danny the Champion of the World
To identify main ideas drawn from more than one paragraph and summarise these.	✔		✔	✔	✔	✔
To identify how language, structure and presentation contribute to meaning.	✔			✔	✔	✔
To retrieve and record information from non-fiction.	✔		✔		✔	
To participate in discussion about both books that are read to them and those they can read for themselves, taking turns and listening to what others say.	✔				✔	✔
Transcription: Spelling						
To use further prefixes and suffixes and understand how to add them (English Appendix 1).	✔	✔	✔		✔	✔
To spell further homophones.				✔		✔
To spell words that are often misspelled (English Appendix 1).		✔		✔		✔
To place the possessive apostrophe accurately in words with regular plurals (for example, girls', boys') and in words with irregular plurals (for example, children's).		✔	✔			
To use the first two or three letters of a word to check its spelling in a dictionary.						
To write from memory simple sentences, dictated by the teacher, that include words and punctuation taught so far.		✔		✔		✔
Handwriting						
To use the diagonal and horizontal strokes that are needed to join letters and understand which letters, when adjacent to one another, are best left unjoined.						
To increase the legibility, consistency and quality of their handwriting (for example, by ensuring that the downstrokes of letters are parallel and equidistant; that lines of writing are spaced sufficiently so that the ascenders and descenders of letters do not touch).						
Composition						
To discuss writing similar to that which they are planning to write in order to understand and learn from its structure, vocabulary and grammar.	✔	✔	✔	✔	✔	

Curriculum objectives	Bill's New Frock	The Owl Who Was Afraid of the Dark	The Twits	The Iron Man	Diary of a Wimpy Kid	Danny the Champion of the World
To discuss and record ideas.			✓	✓	✓	✓
To compose and rehearse sentences orally (including dialogue), progressively building a varied and rich vocabulary and an increasing range of sentence structures (English Appendix 2).	✓	✓	✓			
To organise paragraphs around a theme.	✓	✓			✓	
In narratives, to create settings, characters and plot.	✓	✓	✓	✓	✓	
In non-narrative material, to use simple organisational devices (for example, headings and subheadings).	✓	✓	✓	✓	✓	✓
To assess the effectiveness of their own and others' writing and suggest improvements.					✓	✓
To propose changes to grammar and vocabulary to improve consistency, including the accurate use of pronouns in sentences.						
To proofread for spelling and punctuation errors.			✓			
To read aloud their own writing, to a group or the whole class, using appropriate intonation and controlling the tone and volume so that the meaning is clear.			✓			

Composition: Grammar, vocabulary and punctuation

Curriculum objectives	Bill's New Frock	The Owl Who Was Afraid of the Dark	The Twits	The Iron Man	Diary of a Wimpy Kid	Danny the Champion of the World
To extend the range of sentences with more than one clause by using a wider range of conjunctions, including 'when', 'if', 'because', 'although'.		✓		✓		✓
To use the present perfect form of verbs in contrast to the past tense.						
To choose nouns or pronouns appropriately for clarity and cohesion and to avoid repetition.				✓		✓
To use conjunctions, adverbs and prepositions to express time and cause.		✓			✓	
To use fronted adverbials.		✓	✓	✓	✓	✓
To learn the grammar for Year 3 in English Appendix 2.	✓	✓	✓	✓	✓	✓
To use commas after fronted adverbials.		✓	✓	✓	✓	✓

Curriculum objectives	Bill's New Frock	The Owl Who Was Afraid of the Dark	The Twits	The Iron Man	Diary of a Wimpy Kid	Danny the Champion of the World
To indicate possession by using the possessive apostrophe with plural nouns.		✔	✔		✔	
To use and punctuate direct speech.	✔	✔	✔	✔	✔	✔
To use and understand the grammatical terminology in English Appendix 2 accurately and appropriately when discussing their writing and reading.	✔			✔	✔	✔
Spoken language						
To listen and respond appropriately to adults and their peers.						
To ask relevant questions to extend their understanding and knowledge.	✔	✔		✔		
To use relevant strategies to build their vocabulary.						
To articulate and justify answers, arguments and opinions.	✔		✔	✔		
To give well-structured descriptions, explanations and narratives for different purposes, including for expressing feelings.		✔		✔		✔
To maintain attention and participate actively in collaborative conversations, staying on topic and initiating and responding to comments.				✔	✔	
To use spoken language to develop understanding through speculating, hypothesising, imagining and exploring ideas.	✔		✔	✔	✔	✔
To speak audibly and fluently with an increasing command of Standard English.		✔				
To participate in discussions, presentations, performances, role play, improvisations and debates.	✔	✔	✔	✔	✔	✔
To gain, maintain and monitor the interest of the listeners.						
To consider and evaluate different viewpoints, attending to and building on the contributions of others.	✔	✔		✔	✔	✔
To select and use appropriate registers for effective communication.		✔				

Year 4

Autumn Term 1

George's Marvellous Medicine

Page 43

Autumn Term 2

Why the Whales Came

Page 44

Spring Term 1

Stig of the Dump

Page 45

Spring Term 2

Hetty Feather

Page 46

Summer Term 1

Millions

Page 47

Summer Term 2

How to Train Your Dragon

Page 48

Curriculum objectives
Pages 49–52

George's Marvellous Medicine:
Overview

- ### Topic links
  Roald Dahl

- ### Curriculum links
  PSHE

- ### Text types covered
  Information
  Narrative
  Poetry
  Drama
  Book review
  Instructions

- ### By the same author
  The BFG (Puffin)
  Danny the Champion of the World (Puffin)
  Charlie and the Chocolate Factory (Puffin)
  Matilda (Puffin)
  The Twits (Puffin)
  The Enormous Crocodile (Puffin)

- ### Alternative books
  The Twits, by Roald Dahl (Puffin)

Plot

When George Kranky is left alone with his mean and bad-tempered Grandma on Saturday morning, he decides to create his own version of her 11 o'clock medicine. Using almost every liquid in the house, he concocts a brew which he plans to use to turn her into a nice person. In reality, it turns her into a giant and when George's parents arrive home, Grandma is sticking out of the roof. George's father starts a frenzy of medicine-making which ends with Grandma disappearing.

About the book

George's Marvellous Medicine is a delightful fantasy about a dysfunctional family. There are great lists of ingredients and the usual delight in language that you would expect from a Roald Dahl novel. We have our usual Dahl villain, but who is it: Grandma or Mr Kranky? Grandma was unpleasant but did the punishment fit the crime?

About the teacher's guide

As well as detailed Guided and Shared reading, *Read & Respond: George's Marvellous Medicine* provides the following activities to cover the English curriculum.

Word reading and spelling

- practising using prefixes
- spelling more homophones

Comprehension

- asking questions about George's plan
- inferring how George's feelings change over the day
- comparing themes across other books by Dahl
- talking about the characters' motivations
- discussing the impact of direct speech
- enjoying the vocabulary and use of language

Composition

- using fronted adverbials; using possessive apostrophes
- writing a new ending
- planning a sequel
- writing a book review
- writing a recipe for some marvellous medicine

Speaking and listening

- learning George's chants and discussing how they change the tone of the story
- asking questions about George: is he good or bad?
- asking questions about Grandma: why is she so mean?
- retelling their own version of the story
- debating statements about the book

Why the Whales Came:

Overview

◉ Topic links

Islands

First World War

The sea

◉ Curriculum links

Geography – locational knowledge; human and physical geography

History – local history study

PSHE

◉ Text types covered

Advert

Information

Narrative

Newspaper

◉ By the same author

The Wreck of the Zanzibar (Egmont)

Kensuke's Kingdom (Egmont)

War Horse (Egmont)

The Butterfly Lion (Egmont)

Private Peaceful (Egmont)

The Amazing Story of Adolphus Tips (HarperCollins)

◉ Alternative books

Katie Morag and the Two Grandmothers, by Mairi Hedderwick (Red Fox)

Kensuke's Kingdom, by Michael Morpurgo (Egmont)

Plot

All the children of the island of Bryher know that that they should not talk to the Birdman, but when Gracie and Daniel meet him, they form a firm friendship. Gracie's father joins up to serve in the First World War, but when he goes missing in action the children think it is due to the curse of Samson Island. When narwhals come to Bryher and the villagers want to kill them, Gracie and Daniel must take sides with the Birdman against their families. Their bravery saves the narwhals and perhaps Gracie's father.

About the book

This haunting tale of suspicion and trust is set on the very real island of Bryher (Isles of Scilly) during the start of the First World War. The characters must unpick truth from lies and find out who the heroes of the island really are.

About the teacher's guide

As well as detailed Guided and Shared reading, *Read & Respond: Why the Whales Came* provides the following activities to cover the English curriculum.

Word reading and spelling

- spelling homophones
- writing dictated sentences

Comprehension

- enjoying the island setting
- asking questions and inferring feelings
- looking at turning points
- discussing truth versus freedom
- discussing different themes

Composition

- using pronouns and conjunctions to improve writing
- using fronted adverbials and direct speech
- describing getting lost in the fog
- writing a newspaper article about famine on Samson
- creating a radio play

Speaking and listening

- discussing island life
- practising sign language
- role-playing scenes

Stig of the Dump:

Overview

◉ Topic links

Stone Age
1960s
Recycling

◉ Curriculum links

History – Stone Age; 1960s
PSHE
Design and technology
Art and design
Science – recycling

◉ Text types covered

Diary
Information
Playscript
Poetry
Report
Narrative

◉ By the same author

The Town that Went South
(Atheneum)
Me and my Million (Puffin)
The Night the Water Came (Puffin)

◉ Alternative books

Skellig, by David Almond (Hodder)
The Iron Man, by Ted Hughes
(Faber & Faber)
Why the Whales Came, by Michael
Morpurgo (Egmont)
Mr Stink, by David Walliams
(HarperCollins)

Plot

Barney meets a Neolithic man living in an abandoned, rubbish-filled chalk pit. Stig is virtually an alien to Barney, but they find a way to communicate and build a friendship. Stig is resourceful and quick-thinking and, together, Barney and Stig outsmart a gang, discover burglars, meet an escaped leopard, attend a fancy dress party, and travel back to Stig's own time.

About the book

Stig of the Dump introduces the children to two historical periods: the Stone Age and the 1960s – with different attitudes to freedom, smoking, hunting and animals. Barney learns about trust and friendship, and has some of his assumptions about the Stone Age quashed.

About the teacher's guide

As well as detailed Guided and Shared reading, *Read & Respond: Stig of the Dump* provides the following activities to cover the English curriculum.

Word reading and spelling

- adding suffixes and prefixes to root words

Comprehension

- understanding the transcription of non-standard English and discussing its use in a story
- exploring the chalk pit with Barney
- investigating Stig's use of thrown-away items
- tracking the development of Stig and Barney's friendship
- exploring the chapter structure of home–Stig–home
- evaluating different ways of indicating time and seasons

Composition

- using conjunctions to show time and cause
- using the possessive apostrophe
- writing a seasonal poem
- writing a police report
- creating settings and describing characters

Speaking and listening

- participating in a debate about hunting
- creating and presenting items made from recycled materials
- using hot-seating and improvisation to learn about character
- retelling the story

Hetty Feather:

Overview

Topic links

Victorians

Curriculum links

History – Victorians
Geography – London
PSHE

Text types covered

Information
Narrative
Book review

By the same author

Katy (Puffin)

The Suitcase Kid (Yearling)

Further stories about Hetty Feather (*Sapphire Battersea, Emerald Star, Diamond, Little Stars,* published by Yearling/Corgi)

Alternative books

Cliffhanger, by Jacqueline Wilson (Yearling)

Street Child, by Berlie Doherty (HarperCollins)

A Little Princess, by Frances Hodgson Burnett (Wordsworth)

Plot

Hetty's destitute mother is forced to leave her at a Foundling Hospital. At first she lives with a loving foster family, but back at the Foundling Hospital life is harder. However, she remains upbeat, makes friends, is true to herself and continues to search for her mother.

About the book

Hetty Feather has a wonderfully realised Victorian setting, from family life, school life, the life of the poor – and even circus life. Themes of love, rejection, family, friendship, imagination and being true to yourself are explored through the book. This, the first novel about Hetty, is a great book for asking questions, making inferences, picking up clues and evaluating behaviour.

About the teacher's guide

As well as detailed Guided and Shared reading, *Read & Respond: Hetty Feather* provides the following activities to cover the English curriculum.

Word reading and spelling

- practising prefixes and suffixes
- spelling homophones

Comprehension

- inferring meaning, predicting events and discussing themes
- understanding the historical context of Victorian London
- asking questions and picking up clues
- exploring the meaning of new vocabulary

Composition

- using conjunctions and fronted adverbials
- using and punctuating direct speech
- rewriting a section from another point of view
- developing a non-fiction text on the Foundling Hospital
- planning a sequel
- writing a new ending

Speaking and listening

- hot-seating the different characters
- debating Hetty's thoughts on running away
- delivering a spoken retelling of a key part of the book
- creating tableaux showing clear facial expressions

Millions:

Overview

● Topic links

Families

Water

Trade

● Curriculum links

Mathematics – money

RE – lives of saints

Geography – developing countries

PSHE

● Text types covered

Instructions

Information

Advert

Book review

Diary

Narrative

● By the same author

The Astounding Broccoli Boy
(Macmillan)

Framed (Macmillan)

Cosmic (Macmillan)

Sputnik's Guide to Life on Earth
(Macmillan)

● Alternative books

Billionaire Boy, by David Walliams
(HarperCollins)

The Boy in the Dress, by David
Walliams (HarperCollins)

Plot

God appears to have given brothers Damian and Anthony a bag containing a huge amount of money. Desperate to spend the money before the euro replaces the pound, they start spending inordinate amounts of cash at school as well as donating it to charity. Soon people become suspicious – including the people whose money it is. While trying to cope with their sudden and unexpected wealth, the two boys grieve for their dead mother and come to terms with a busy father and a new home.

About the book

Millions is a very successful mix of fantasy (becoming suddenly rich; having saints talk directly to you), adventure story (who will end up with the money?) and a story that raises issues (new home, working father, grieving for a lost mother). It is alternatively funny, exciting and sad.

About the teacher's guide

As well as detailed Guided and Shared reading, *Read & Respond: Millions* provides the following activities to cover the English curriculum.

Word reading and spelling

• spelling homophones
• spelling words with prefixes

Comprehension

• understanding new words
• discussing the themes of grief, families, greed
• discussing the use of non-fiction extracts in the novel
• using actions and reactions to discuss what Dorothy is like
• drawing up a list of questions for the author

Composition

• using conjunctions to improve sentences
• using direct speech, fronted adverbials and possessive phrases
• using estate agent jargon to write a house advert
• writing a book review
• writing a story about having a million pounds
• writing a new ending for the story
• writing a diary entry including similes and metaphors

Speaking and listening

• discussing the story from Anthony's viewpoint
• role-playing a new scene from the book
• discussing how difficult it is to be good
• creating a present-day saint for their classmates to vote for
• sharing experiences of imaginary friends
• role-playing a conversation from the book

How to Train Your Dragon:

Overview

- **Topic links**
  - Island life
  - Vikings
  - Dragons

- **Curriculum links**
  - **Science** – animals
  - **Geography** – islands
  - **History** – Vikings

- **Text types covered**
  - Information
  - Fact file
  - Event poster
  - Book review
  - Narrative
  - Poetry
  - Letter

- **By the same author**
  - *That Rabbit Belongs to Emily Brown* (Hodder)
  - *Hiccup the Viking Who Was Seasick* (Hodder)

- **Alternative books**
  - *The Saga of Erik the Viking*, by Terry Jones (Puffin)
  - *Hiccup the Viking Who Was Seasick*, by Cressida Cowell (Hodder)
  - *Diary of a Wimpy Kid*, by Jeff Kinney (Puffin)

Plot

Hiccup Horrendous Haddock the Third is a bit of a weed, which is a shame because he is son of the chief and about to start his Viking training with nine other boys. First they must catch their dragon and then train their dragon. Hiccup's dragon seems as pathetic as he does but, amazingly, when the tribe really needs a hero to save them from a vicious sea dragon, Hiccup and Toothless rise to the challenge.

About the book

How to Train Your Dragon is a hugely entertaining adventure story with a panoply of larger-than-life characters, from Stoick the Vast (Oh Hear his Name and Tremble Ug Ug) to mean-spirited Snotlout. The adventures are illustrated with wild child-like drawings and enhanced with a dragon fact file. Informal language abounds as well as quite a few politically incorrect thought processes (on behalf of the Vikings).

About the teacher's guide

As well as detailed Guided and Shared reading, *Read & Respond: How to Train Your Dragon* provides the following activities to cover the English curriculum.

Word reading and spelling
- spelling words with prefixes

Comprehension
- discussing interesting words and phrases
- finding and discussing themes (family, tradition, danger)
- summarising the plot and finding main ideas
- asking questions about Vikings
- inferring feelings and predicting events

Composition
- using 'a'/'an', possessives, plurals and capitals
- creating a poster for a Viking festival
- writing a book review for another book in the series
- making notes from non-fiction
- writing dialogue for a new scene
- writing and performing a song
- writing a letter of complaint from one of the characters

Speaking and listening
- telling stories
- interviewing Hiccup
- providing different characters' opinions on heroes
- practising delivering jokes
- debating different dilemmas in the book

Curriculum objectives	George's Marvellous Medicine	Why the Whales Came	Stig of the Dump	Hetty Feather	Millions	How to Train Your Dragon
Word reading						
To apply their growing knowledge of root words, prefixes and suffixes (etymology and morphology) as listed in English Appendix 1, both to read aloud and to understand the meaning of new words they meet.	✓	✓	✓	✓	✓	✓
To read further exception words, noting the unusual correspondences between spelling and sound, and where these occur in the word.						
Comprehension						
To develop positive attitudes to reading and an understanding of what they read.		✓			✓	✓
To listen to and discuss a wide range of fiction, poetry, plays, non-fiction and reference books or textbooks.			✓		✓	
To read books that are structured in different ways and read for a range of purposes.	✓	✓		✓		
To use dictionaries to check the meaning of words that they have read.				✓	✓	
To increase their familiarity with a wide range of books, including fairy stories, myths and legends, and retell some of these orally.						
To identify themes and conventions in a wide range of books.	✓	✓	✓	✓	✓	✓
To prepare poems and playscripts to read aloud and to perform, showing understanding through intonation, tone, volume and action.	✓	✓			✓	
To discuss words and phrases that capture the reader's interest and imagination.	✓	✓		✓		✓
To recognise some different forms of poetry (for example, free verse, narrative poetry).						
To check that the text makes sense to them, discussing their understanding and explaining the meaning of words in context.				✓	✓	✓
To ask questions to improve their understanding of a text.	✓	✓	✓	✓	✓	
To draw inferences such as inferring characters' feelings, thoughts and motives from their actions, and justify inferences with evidence.	✓	✓	✓	✓	✓	✓
To predict what might happen from details stated and implied.	✓		✓	✓	✓	✓

Curriculum objectives	George's Marvellous Medicine	Why the Whales Came	Stig of the Dump	Hetty Feather	Millions	How to Train Your Dragon
To identify main ideas drawn from more than one paragraph and summarise these.		✓	✓		✓	✓
To identify how language, structure and presentation contribute to meaning.	✓	✓	✓		✓	✓
To retrieve and record information from non-fiction.		✓		✓		✓
To participate in discussion about both books that are read to them and those they can read for themselves, taking turns and listening to what others say.				✓		
Transcription: Spelling						
To use further prefixes and suffixes and understand how to add them (English Appendix 1).	✓		✓	✓	✓	✓
To spell further homophones.	✓	✓		✓	✓	
To spell words that are often misspelled (English Appendix 1).						
To place the possessive apostrophe accurately in words with regular plurals (for example, girls', boys') and in words with irregular plurals (for example, children's).	✓		✓		✓	✓
To use the first two or three letters of a word to check its spelling in a dictionary.						
To write from memory simple sentences, dictated by the teacher, that include words and punctuation taught so far.		✓				✓
Handwriting						
To use the diagonal and horizontal strokes that are needed to join letters and understand which letters, when adjacent to one another, are best left unjoined.						
To increase the legibility, consistency and quality of their handwriting (for example, by ensuring that the downstrokes of letters are parallel and equidistant; that lines of writing are spaced sufficiently so that the ascenders and descenders of letters do not touch).						
Composition						
To discuss writing similar to that which they are planning to write in order to understand and learn from its structure, vocabulary and grammar.	✓	✓	✓		✓	✓

Year 4

Curriculum objectives	George's Marvellous Medicine	Why the Whales Came	Stig of the Dump	Hetty Feather	Millions	How to Train Your Dragon
To discuss and record ideas.	✓	✓	✓	✓	✓	
To compose and rehearse sentences orally (including dialogue), progressively building a varied and rich vocabulary and an increasing range of sentence structures (English Appendix 2).	✓		✓	✓		
To organise paragraphs around a theme.	✓	✓	✓		✓	✓
In narratives, to create settings, characters and plot.	✓	✓	✓	✓	✓	✓
In non-narrative material, to use simple organisational devices (for example, headings and subheadings).	✓	✓		✓	✓	✓
To assess the effectiveness of their own and others' writing and suggest improvements.				✓	✓	✓
To propose changes to grammar and vocabulary to improve consistency, including the accurate use of pronouns in sentences.						
To proofread for spelling and punctuation errors.						✓
To read aloud their own writing, to a group or the whole class, using appropriate intonation and controlling the tone and volume so that the meaning is clear.						✓
Composition: Grammar, vocabulary and punctuation						
To extend the range of sentences with more than one clause by using a wider range of conjunctions, including 'when', 'if', 'because', 'although'.	✓	✓		✓	✓	✓
To use the present perfect form of verbs in contrast to the past tense.						
To choose nouns or pronouns appropriately for clarity and cohesion and to avoid repetition.	✓	✓		✓		
To use conjunctions, adverbs and prepositions to express time and cause.			✓			✓
To use fronted adverbials.	✓	✓		✓	✓	
To learn the grammar for Year 4 in English Appendix 2.	✓	✓	✓	✓	✓	✓
To use commas after fronted adverbials.	✓	✓		✓	✓	

Year 4

Curriculum objectives	George's Marvellous Medicine	Why the Whales Came	Stig of the Dump	Hetty Feather	Millions	How to Train Your Dragon
To indicate possession by using the possessive apostrophe with plural nouns.	✓			✓	✓	
To use and punctuate direct speech.	✓	✓	✓	✓	✓	✓
To use and understand the grammatical terminology in English Appendix 2 accurately and appropriately when discussing their writing and reading.	✓	✓	✓	✓	✓	✓
Spoken language						
To listen and respond appropriately to adults and their peers.						
To ask relevant questions to extend their understanding and knowledge.						✓
To use relevant strategies to build their vocabulary.						
To articulate and justify answers, arguments and opinions.		✓			✓	
To give well-structured descriptions, explanations and narratives for different purposes, including for expressing feelings.	✓			✓		✓
To maintain attention and participate actively in collaborative conversations, staying on topic and initiating and responding to comments.				✓		
To use spoken language to develop understanding through speculating, hypothesising, imagining and exploring ideas.	✓	✓		✓	✓	✓
To speak audibly and fluently with an increasing command of Standard English.						
To participate in discussions, presentations, performances, role play, improvisations and debates.	✓	✓	✓	✓	✓	✓
To gain, maintain and monitor the interest of the listeners.			✓			✓
To consider and evaluate different viewpoints, attending to and building on the contributions of others.		✓	✓		✓	✓
To select and use appropriate registers for effective communication.	✓		✓			

Year 5

Autumn Term 1

Kensuke's Kingdom

Page 54

Autumn Term 2

Charlie and the Chocolate Factory

Page 55

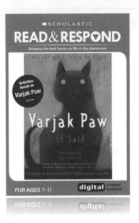

Spring Term 1

Varjak Paw

Page 56

Spring Term 2

Holes

Page 57

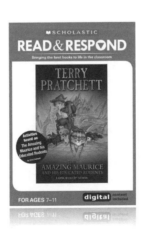

Summer Term 1

The Amazing Maurice and His Educated Rodents

Page 58

Summer Term 2

War Horse

Page 59

Curriculum objectives
Pages 60–64

Kensuke's Kingdom:

Overview

Topic links
Islands
Rainforests

Curriculum links
Geography – islands
Geography – maps
History – Second World War
Science – animals/ecology

Text types covered
Newspaper article
Narrative
Persuasive
Diary
Instructions
Letter

By the same author
War Horse (Egmont)
Why the Whales Came (Egmont)
The Wreck of the Zanzibar (Egmont)
Private Peaceful (Egmont)

Alternative books
Why the Whales Came, by Michael Morpurgo (Egmont)
The Great Kapok Tree, by Lynne Cherry (Harcourt Brace)

Plot

When Michael falls overboard while his family are sailing around the world, he becomes marooned on an island in the Philippines. He soon realises that he's not alone – the island is inhabited by an old Japanese man called Kensuke, who has lived there since his family died in Nagasaki at the end of the Second World War. Together they fish, play football, watch turtles laying eggs and protect orang-utans from hunters. Finally, Michael's parents arrive to rescue him.

About the book

This classic adventure story of a boy stranded on a desert island is made into a safe fantasy with the help of a grandfather figure. The mix of history, science and geography, fantastic description, exciting adventure and touching friendship make a thoroughly enjoyable read and a perfect book for Key Stage 2.

About the teacher's guide

As well as detailed Guided and Shared reading, *Read & Respond: Kensuke's Kingdom* provides the following activities to cover the English curriculum.

Word reading and spelling
- spelling homophones

Comprehension
- understanding synonyms and antonyms
- plotting Michael's journey on a map and inferring his feelings
- understanding the key roles of animals in the book
- making notes from an article
- understanding key relationships and predicting how it might develop
- summarising key events
- investigating cause and effect

Composition
- using the passive voice, formal and informal writing
- using relative clauses and linking paragraphs
- writing a diary and a letter
- considering an alternative ending
- writing descriptive passages using the senses

Speaking and listening
- discussing the progress of time
- asking questions about the story
- participating in a role play
- choosing a format and giving a presentation
- discussing forms of communication

Charlie and the Chocolate Factory:
Overview

Topic links
Chocolate

Curriculum links
Art and design

Text types covered
Information
Narrative
Poetry
Book review
Instructions

By the same author
The BFG (Puffin)
Danny the Champion of the World (Puffin)
George's Marvellous Medicine (Puffin)
Matilda (Puffin)
The Twits (Puffin)
The Enormous Crocodile (Puffin)

Alternative books
George's Marvellous Medicine, by Roald Dahl (Puffin)

Plot

When Charlie Bucket finds a golden ticket in a chocolate bar, he joins Augustus Gloop, Veruca Salt, Mike Teavee and Violet Beauregarde for a tour around Willy Wonka's chocolate factory. Every imaginable form of sweet and chocolate can be seen in the magical factory but only Charlie is able to follow the rules. One by one the other children fall foul of their greed until only Charlie is left and his prize is the chocolate factory itself.

About the book

This ultimate fantasy of chocolate and sweets is a masterful piece of imaginative writing that entices the senses. Normal, kind, quiet, selfless Charlie is surrounded by exotic cartoon-like characters, not least the magical but dangerous Willy Wonka. But at its centre there is a strong message about greed versus gratitude and good versus bad behaviour. News reports, songs and bizarre dialogue create a literary delight.

About the teacher's guide

As well as detailed Guided and Shared reading, *Read & Respond: Charlie and the Chocolate Factory* provides the following activities to cover the English curriculum.

Word reading and spelling
- spelling a range of words with silent letters
- spelling more homophones

Comprehension
- using prediction and questions to engage with the text
- using dialogue to understand character
- using actions to infer feelings
- enjoying the names of the characters

Composition
- using modal verbs and the passive voice
- using commas, semi-colons, colons and dashes
- practising précising skills
- writing new poems in the style of the Oompa-Loompas
- writing non-fiction text about modern chocolate-making
- writing a book review

Speaking and listening
- performing the songs of the Oompa-Loompas
- hot-seating characters
- debating Charlie's dilemma about spending money
- practising storytelling skills

Varjak Paw:

Overview

◉ Topic links

Cats

Egypt and Mesopotamia

◉ Curriculum links

Art and design

PSHE

History – Ancient Sumer

◉ Text types covered

Information

Myths

Poetry

Playscript

Comic strip

Narrative

Report

◉ By the same author

The Outlaw Varjak Paw (Corgi)

Phoenix (Corgi)

◉ Alternative books

Gobbolino the Witch's Cat, by Ursula Moray Williams (Puffin)

I Was a Rat, by Philip Pullman (Yearling)

The Owl Who Was Afraid of the Dark, by Jill Tomlinson (Egmont)

Plot

Varjak Paw, a Mesopotamian Blue kitten, hears stories about the Way of Jalal – a secret martial art that uses Slow-Time, Moving Circles and Shadow-Walking. When danger arrives at home, Varjak escapes outside and goes into the brutal city of fighting cat gangs and wild dogs. Here he dreams of ancient Mesopotamia, learns the Way and finds out who he truly is. With a new friend, Holly, they investigate the mysterious Vanishings.

About the book

With contrasting settings (the house, the city, Mesopotamia) and characters (pedigree and feral cats and dogs, sinister humans) and rich descriptive language, *Varjak Paw* is a very sensory adventure story. As Varjak learns from dreams and reality, he has to discover the truth and learn about bravery, friendship and the real value of a cat.

About the teacher's guide

As well as detailed Guided and Shared reading, *Read & Respond: Varjak Paw* provides the following activities to cover the English curriculum.

Word reading and spelling

- practising words with prefixes
- spelling further homophones

Comprehension

- investigating how the author builds cohesion
- discussing the impact and skill of the illustrations
- investigating how the author creates distinct characters
- using story dialogue to create a drama
- exploring the Mesopotamian dream setting
- understanding the theme of coming of age

Composition

- using dashes, colons and commas
- using relative clauses
- creating a comic strip of a scene
- using the author's sensory techniques to write a new scene
- using evidence from the text to write a crime report
- writing a diary in the voice of Varjak

Speaking and listening

- using story maps to retell parts of the story
- debating 'Cats versus Dogs'
- presenting group thoughts on the book's themes

Holes:

Overview

- **Topic links**

  Deserts

- **Curriculum links**

  Geography – deserts
  RE
  Citizenship
  PSHE

- **Text types covered**

  Narrative
  Information
  Rules
  Letters
  Diary

- **By the same author**

  There's a Boy in the Girls' Bathroom
  (Bloomsbury)
  Small Steps (Bloomsbury)

- **Alternative books**

  The Diary of a Killer Cat, by Anne
  Fine (Puffin)

Plot

After an unfortunate incident with a pair of stolen shoes, Stanley, the last in a long line of the unlucky Yelnats family, finds himself at Camp Green Lake Juvenile Detention Centre. The lake is now a dry empty desert and every day the boys must each dig a hole. Soon Stanley realises that the Warden is looking for something. When Stanley and his friend Zero run away they begin to unravel the mystery, and Stanley unconsciously undoes the curse on his family. Not only do they find the treasure, but it turns out to belong to Stanley.

About the book

With language as sparse as the landscape, *Holes* does not have a word out of place. The straight talking captures the resignation of Stanley Yelnats and the bizarre and unique story needs no wow words or complex description to detract from its atmosphere and action (a fantastic contrast to the exuberance of Roald Dahl). Five key events in the history of the characters interweave, raising issues of race, poverty, family, bullies, personal development, friendship and destiny. American spelling and vocabulary offer interesting vocabulary work.

About the teacher's guide

As well as detailed Guided and Shared reading, *Read & Respond: Holes* provides the following activities to cover the English curriculum.

Word reading and spelling

- using a dictionary and thesaurus
- spelling words that need to be learned

Comprehension

- describing settings, characters and atmosphere
- understanding American English
- understanding superstition, curses and destiny in the story
- investigating the weaving together of different stories

Composition

- using the passive voice
- using relative clauses and their punctuation
- writing a letter from Stanley
- creating an obituary for Kate Barlow
- describing a new deadly animal

Speaking and listening

- clearly describing a chain of events
- presentation on the dangers of the desert
- role-playing a scene to understand the racism of the story

The Amazing Maurice and His Educated Rodents:
Overview

- **Topic links**

  Fantasy stories

  Famous authors

- **Curriculum links**

  Art and design

- **Text types covered**

  Information

  Narrative

  Drama

- **By the same author**

  The Colour of Magic (Corgi)

  The Wee Free Men (Corgi)

  A Hat Full of Sky (Corgi)

  I Shall Wear Midnight (Corgi)

- **Alternative books**

  Truckers, by Terry Pratchett (Corgi)

  Igraine the Brave, by Cornelia Funke (Chicken House)

Plot

Maurice (a cat and a con artist) has created a living tricking villagers, using a pack of enchanted rats and a young (human) piper called Keith. However, there is dissent in the ranks as the rats (worried about the morality), Keith (wants to play the flute) and Maurice (wants all the money) all have different hopes for their final trick. Unfortunately, the people of Bad Blintz are not easy to trick...

About the book

The Amazing Maurice and His Educated Rodents is a parody of the fairy tale of 'The Pied Piper of Hamelin'. It is funny and fantastical, with bizarre characters and silly names, but it also raises ethical issues and dilemmas to discuss. There is also fear in the cellars and drainpipes. The novel is a children's book that fits into Terry Pratchett's *Discworld* fantasy series for adults and will hopefully inspire readers to challenge themselves to read on in the series.

About the teacher's guide

As well as detailed Guided and Shared reading, *Read & Respond: The Amazing Maurice and His Educated Rodents* provides the following activities to cover the English curriculum.

Word reading and spelling

- spelling words with silent letters
- adding suffixes

Comprehension

- taking notes during a first reading
- asking questions of the text
- discussing and enjoying the character names
- inferring feelings and character
- discussing the theme of leadership

Composition

- using passive verbs
- using more sophisticated punctuation for clarity
- writing a story with a simple theme
- planning a sequel for the story
- writing a review for the novel
- writing a new ending

Speaking and listening

- hot-seating different characters
- role playing two characters meeting
- debating on who the new leader should be
- using notes to tell a version of the last day
- creating a debate between Maurice and his conscience

War Horse:

Overview

- ◉ **Topic links**
  First World War

- ◉ **Curriculum links**
  History – First World War
  PSHE

- ◉ **Text types covered**
  Information
  Persuasive
  Letter
  Poetry
  Narrative
  Report

- ◉ **By the same author**
  Private Peaceful (HarperCollins)
  Farm Boy (HarperCollins)
  An Eagle in the Snow (HarperCollins)
  The Mozart Question (Walker Books)

- ◉ **Alternative books**
  War Game, by Michael Foreman
  (Pavilion)
  Why the Whales Came, by Michael
  Morpurgo (Walker Books)

Plot

When a farmer buys a half-thoroughbred colt in an auction, the young horse forms a strong friendship with the farmer's son, Albert. Albert trains Joey to work on the farm, but Joey is requisitioned by the army. Albert joins up as soon as he's old enough and travels to France, where he hopes to meet Joey. Meanwhile, Joey, mentored by another horse called Topthorn, sees the war as he is used/cared for by an English captain, a French girl and a German soldier in succession. After he becomes trapped in no man's land, he is freed by a German and an English soldier working together. Back at a hospital he is reunited with Albert.

About the book

A classic of our time, made famous by film and stage play, *War Horse* movingly views the horrors of the First World War through the eyes of a horse. As Joey is looked after by different people we see how the war destroys lives on either side – and for those stuck in the middle.

About the teacher's guide

As well as detailed Guided and Shared reading, *Read & Respond: War Horse* provides the following activities to cover the English curriculum.

Word reading and spelling

- spelling words with the suffixes 'ible', 'able' and 'ough'

Comprehension

- tracking the theme of friendship
- appreciating how the war is described
- understanding the historical background
- investigating different points of view

Composition

- using modal verbs
- building cohesion and using the best punctuation for clarity
- creating a sense of time passing quickly
- writing a non-rhyming poem inspired by the subject
- writing a reply to Trooper Warren's letter
- writing reminiscences of Joey's time at war
- writing an officer's log
- practising précising

Speaking and listening

- hot-seating the characters
- creating a role play set in the trenches
- debating the rights and wrongs of war
- discussing a recruiting poster

Year 5

Curriculum objectives	Kensuke's Kingdom	Charlie and the Chocolate Factory	Varjak Paw	Holes	The Amazing Maurice and His Educated Rodents	War Horse
Word reading						
To apply their growing knowledge of root words, prefixes and suffixes (etymology and morphology) as listed in English Appendix 1, both to read aloud and to understand the meaning of new words they meet.	✓	✓	✓	✓	✓	✓
Comprehension						
To maintain positive attitudes to reading and understanding of what they read.	✓		✓	✓		
To continue to read and discuss an increasingly wide range of fiction, poetry, plays, non-fiction and reference books or textbooks.						
To read books that are structured in different ways and read for a range of purposes.		✓			✓	
To increase their familiarity with a wide range of books, including myths, legends and traditional stories, modern fiction, fiction from our literary heritage, and books from other cultures and traditions.					✓	
To recommend books that they have read to their peers, giving reasons for their choices.		✓				✓
To identify and discuss themes and conventions in and across a wide range of writing.		✓	✓	✓	✓	✓
To make comparisons within and across books.				✓		
To learn a wider range of poetry by heart.						
To prepare poems and plays to read aloud and to perform, showing understanding through intonation, tone and volume so that the meaning is clear to an audience.		✓				
To check that the text makes sense to them, discussing their understanding and explaining the meaning of words in context.		✓		✓	✓	✓
To ask questions to improve their understanding of a text.	✓	✓		✓	✓	✓
To draw inferences such as inferring characters' feelings, thoughts and motives from their actions, and justify inferences with evidence.	✓	✓		✓	✓	✓
To predict what might happen from details stated and implied.	✓	✓	✓	✓	✓	
To summarise the main ideas drawn from more than one paragraph, identifying key details that support the main ideas.	✓		✓	✓	✓	✓

Year 5

Curriculum objectives	Kensuke's Kingdom	Charlie and the Chocolate Factory	Varjak Paw	Holes	The Amazing Maurice and His Educated Rodents	War Horse
To identify how language, structure, and presentation contribute to meaning.			✔	✔		✔
To discuss and evaluate how authors use language, including figurative language, considering the impact on the reader.	✔	✔		✔	✔	✔
To distinguish between statements of fact and opinion.		✔		✔	✔	
To retrieve, record and present information from non-fiction.	✔			✔		✔
To participate in discussions about books that are read to them and those they can read for themselves, building on their own and others' ideas and challenging views courteously.						
To explain and discuss their understanding of what they have read, including through formal presentations and debates, maintaining a focus on the topic and using notes where necessary.			✔	✔		
To provide reasoned justifications for their views.				✔		
Transcription: Spelling						
To use further prefixes and suffixes and understand the guidance for adding them.			✔		✔	✔
To spell some words with 'silent' letters (for example, knight, psalm, solemn).		✔			✔	
To continue to distinguish between homophones and other words which are often confused.	✔	✔	✔	✔	✔	
To use knowledge of morphology and etymology in spelling and understand that the spelling of some words needs to be learned specifically, as listed in English Appendix 1.	✔			✔		✔
To use dictionaries to check the spelling and meaning of words.				✔		
To use the first three or four letters of a word to check spelling, meaning or both of these in a dictionary.						
To use a thesaurus.				✔		
Handwriting						
To write legibly, fluently and with increasing speed.						

Curriculum objectives	Kensuke's Kingdom	Charlie and the Chocolate Factory	Varjak Paw	Holes	The Amazing Maurice and His Educated Rodents	War Horse
To choose which shape of a letter to use when given choices and decide whether or not to join specific letters.						
To choose the writing implement that is best suited for a task.						
Composition						
To identify the audience for and purpose of the writing, selecting the appropriate form and using other similar writing as models for their own.	✔	✔	✔	✔	✔	
To note and develop initial ideas, drawing on reading and research where necessary.					✔	
In writing narratives, to consider how authors have developed characters and settings in what pupils have read, listened to or seen performed.		✔	✔			
To select appropriate grammar and vocabulary, understanding how such choices can change and enhance meaning.	✔		✔		✔	✔
In narratives, to describe settings, characters and atmosphere and integrate dialogue to convey character and advance the action.	✔		✔	✔	✔	✔
To précis longer passages.	✔	✔		✔	✔	✔
To use a wide range of devices to build cohesion within and across paragraphs.	✔		✔			✔
To use further organisational and presentational devices to structure text and to guide the reader (for example, headings, bullet points, underlining).		✔	✔	✔		✔
To assess the effectiveness of their own and others' writing.		✔	✔	✔		
To propose changes to vocabulary, grammar and punctuation to enhance effects and clarify meaning.			✔			
To ensure the consistent and correct use of tense throughout a piece of writing.	✔					
To ensure correct subject and verb agreement when using singular and plural, distinguishing between the language of speech and writing and choosing the appropriate register.		✔				
To proofread for spelling and punctuation errors.						
To perform their own compositions, using appropriate intonation, volume, and movement so that meaning is clear.						

Year 5

Curriculum objectives	Kensuke's Kingdom	Charlie and the Chocolate Factory	Varjak Paw	Holes	The Amazing Maurice and His Educated Rodents	War Horse
Composition: Grammar, vocabulary and punctuation						
To recognise vocabulary and structures that are appropriate for formal speech and writing, including subjunctive forms.	✓		✓	✓		
To use passive verbs to affect the presentation of information in a sentence.	✓	✓		✓	✓	
To use the perfect form of verbs to mark relationships of time and cause.						
To use expanded noun phrases to convey complicated information concisely.			✓			
To use modal verbs or adverbs to indicate degrees of possibility.			✓		✓	✓
To use relative clauses beginning with 'who', 'which', 'where', 'when', 'whose', 'that' or with an implied (omitted) relative pronoun.	✓	✓	✓	✓		
To learn the grammar for Year 5 in English Appendix 2.	✓	✓	✓	✓	✓	✓
To use commas to clarify meaning or avoid ambiguity in writing.		✓	✓	✓	✓	
To use hyphens to avoid ambiguity.					✓	
To use brackets, dashes or commas to indicate parenthesis.			✓			✓
To use semi-colons, colons or dashes to mark boundaries between independent clauses.	✓	✓			✓	✓
To use a colon to introduce a list.			✓			✓
To punctuate bullet points consistently.						
To use and understand the grammatical terminology in English Appendix 2 accurately and appropriately in discussing their writing and reading.	✓	✓	✓	✓	✓	✓
Spoken language						
To listen and respond appropriately to adults and their peers.						
To ask relevant questions to extend their understanding and knowledge.	✓					✓

Year 5

Curriculum objectives	Kensuke's Kingdom	Charlie and the Chocolate Factory	Varjak Paw	Holes	The Amazing Maurice and His Educated Rodents	War Horse
To use relevant strategies to build their vocabulary.			✓			
To articulate and justify answers, arguments and opinions.						
To give well-structured descriptions, explanations and narratives for different purposes, including for expressing feelings.		✓		✓	✓	✓
To maintain attention and participate actively in collaborative conversations, staying on topic and initiating and responding to comments.	✓	✓	✓		✓	✓
To use spoken language to develop understanding through speculating, hypothesising, imagining and exploring ideas.	✓	✓		✓	✓	
To speak audibly and fluently with an increasing command of Standard English.						
To participate in discussions, presentations, performances, role play, improvisations and debates.	✓	✓	✓	✓	✓	✓
To gain, maintain and monitor the interest of the listeners.	✓		✓	✓		
To consider and evaluate different viewpoints, attending to and building on the contributions of others.	✓			✓		
To select and use appropriate registers for effective communication.			✓	✓		

Year 6

Autumn Term 1

Charlotte's Web

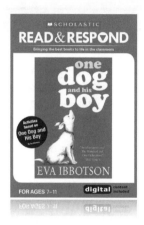

Autumn Term 2

One Dog and His Boy

Spring Term 1

Carrie's War

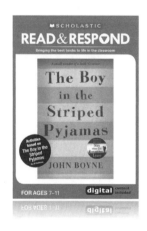

Spring Term 2

The Boy in the
Striped Pyjamas

Summer Term 1

Goodnight Mister Tom

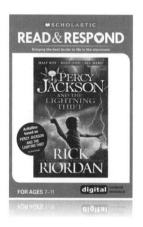

Summer Term 2

Percy Jackson and
the Lightning Thief

Charlotte's Web:

Overview

Topic links

Farms

Curriculum links

Science – animals

Art and design

Citizenship

Geography – human and physical geography

Text types covered

Factfile

Report

Narrative

Interview

Instructions

Diary

By the same author

Stuart Little (HarperCollins)

Alternative books

The Owl Who Was Afraid of the Dark, by Jill Tomlinson (Egmont)

The Sheep-Pig, by Dick King-Smith (Puffin)

Plot

Fern persuades her father to let her keep the smallest pig in the new litter. She names him Wilbur and puts him in the barn. Here, Wilbur meets the other animals including a wise spider called Charlotte and a greedy rat called Templeton. When Wilbur looks fat enough to eat, Charlotte weaves a sign saying 'Some Pig' across the door. Wilbur becomes an attraction rather than bacon. But at the end of the summer, Charlotte, with the help of the other animals, must save Wilbur once more, at the fair. Charlotte dies but leaves new spiderling friends for Wilbur.

About the book

The circle of life, love, loss, friendship, bravery and sacrifice are all here in this much-loved classic. The animals' characters are clearly defined and even the self-serving rat is loveable and ultimately redeems himself.

About the teacher's guide

As well as detailed Guided and Shared reading, *Read & Respond: Charlotte's Web* provides the following activities to cover the English curriculum.

Word reading and spelling

- spelling words with the suffixes 'ible' and 'able'

Comprehension

- discussing the relative importance of the characters
- inferring Templeton's feelings and motives
- mapping the structure of the plot
- discussing Charlotte's sophisticated vocabulary
- locating facts and opinions
- using details to draw the location

Composition

- using modal verbs and formal and informal language
- using more sophisticated punctuation for clarity
- writing a tribute to Charlotte
- using magazines and newspapers to find words to use
- drawing up a set of instructions for baby spiders
- rewriting part of the text with Wilbur as the narrator
- writing a diary entry for Templeton

Speaking and listening

- role-playing an interview with the main characters
- describing events from different perspectives
- retelling a personal experience
- persuasive talk about spiders

One Dog and His Boy:

Overview

● Topic links

Pets

Families

● Curriculum links

PSHE

Art and design

Geography – maps

● Text types covered

Persuasive

Bullet points

Rules

Poetry

Narrative

Postcard

● By the same author

Journey to the River Sea (Macmillan)

The Secret of Platform 13 (Macmillan)

The Star of Kazan (Macmillan)

The Dragonfly Pool (Macmillan)

● Alternative books

The World According to Humphrey, by Betty G Birney (Faber & Faber)

Plot

Poor little rich boy Hal has everything he wants – except affection. When he asks for a pet dog, his parents get him one for the weekend from a dog-rental agency. When his parents return Fleck to the rental agency, Hal goes to get him back. Pippa, working at the agency that day, lets him have Fleck but also releases other dogs, who start to follow Hal. Pippa and Hal go on the run to Hal's grandparents in Northumberland. On the way they find owners for the other dogs.

About the book

One Dog and His Boy teaches us the importance of love over all things. Riches are shown to be pointless unless they can be used to help others. This touching tale of what people will do for love and friendship is also a classic chase story.

About the teacher's guide

As well as detailed Guided and Shared reading, *Read & Respond: One Dog and His Boy* provides the following activities to cover the English curriculum.

Word reading and spelling

- finding and using synonyms and antonyms
- spelling words that need to be learned

Comprehension

- understanding the motivation of the characters
- predicting events and justifying thoughts
- discussing an omniscient narrator and the changing viewpoints
- plotting Hal's journey on a map
- storyboarding a film version
- investigating the problem–resolution structure
- understanding how the author creates suspense
- discussing the different themes in the book

Composition

- using relative clauses, the passive voice and adverbials
- creating a new dog for the agency
- writing rhyming couplets
- writing a postcard from a chosen character
- researching and writing about famous dogs

Speaking and listening

- recounting experiences that link to the text
- discussing the benefits and responsibilities of owning a dog
- articulating the viewpoint of different characters
- debating the rights and wrongs of working dogs and of dogs in circuses

Carrie's War:

Overview

Topic links
Second World War

Curriculum links
History – Second World War
PSHE

Text types covered
Information
Narrative
Diary
Letter

By the same author
The Peppermint Pig (Puffin)

Alternative books
The Lion and the Unicorn, by Shirley Hughes (Red Fox)

War Boy, by Michael Foreman (Pavilion)

Plot

Evacuated to the country during the Second World War, Carrie and her brother lodge with Auntie Lou and her bad-tempered brother Mr Evans. When visiting Mr Evans' other sister Mrs Gotobed at her house, Druid's Bottom, they become friends with an evacuee called Albert, the housekeeper Hepzibah and Mrs Gotobed's disabled cousin Johnny. When Mrs Gotobed dies, her will requests that Hepzibah and Johnny be allowed to stay in the house, but Mr Evans gives them notice to leave. As Carrie departs for home by train she sees Druid's Bottom on fire. She is guilt-stricken as she believes she has caused this by throwing a cursed skull into the pond. However, when Carrie returns thirty years later, she finds Albert has bought the house and Hepzibah and Johnny still live there.

About the book

Carrie's War is a story about memory, nostalgia, guilt, lost opportunities and how we treat each other. It follows the tradition of other evacuation stories where city children find safety, freedom and something magical in the countryside.

About the teacher's guide

As well as detailed Guided and Shared reading, *Read & Respond: Carrie's War* provides the following activities to cover the English curriculum.

Word reading and spelling
- spelling words with 'ough'

Comprehension
- discussing the numerous themes in the book
- exploring the ideas of fear, superstition and legend
- discussing the purpose of the frame of the opening and closing chapters and how Carrie might have changed
- noting how the characters are changed by their experiences
- discussing the tense relationship between Mr Evans and Auntie Lou

Composition
- using modal verbs and choosing the best punctuation
- writing down a memory of their own
- creating a spooky and atmospheric description
- researching and writing a text about rationing

Speaking and listening
- articulating thoughts on being ordinary or peculiar
- role-playing an honest rather than a brave discussion during the war
- discussing different viewpoints of the same event
- role playing being an evacuee

The Boy in the Striped Pyjamas:
Overview

◉ Topic links

Second World War

◉ Curriculum links

History – Second World War
PSHE

◉ Text types covered

Persuasive
Narrative
Biography

◉ By the same author

The Terrible Thing that Happened to Barnaby Brocket (Corgi)

Stay Where You Are and Then Leave (Corgi)

◉ Alternative books

The Mozart Question, by Michael Morpurgo (Walker Books)

The Terrible Thing that Happened to Barnaby Brocket, by John Boyne (Corgi)

The Silver Sword, by Ian Serraillier (Red Fox)

I am David, by Anne Holm (Egmont)

Plot

In the middle of the Second World War, Bruno and his parents move to a house near his father's new work. There is no one for him to play with so Bruno explores the area. He meets a boy in striped pyjamas sitting on the other side of a fence. Bruno visits Shmuel as often as he can. Over the months Shmuel gets thinner. When Bruno has his head shaved, he and Shmuel descide to smuggle Bruno across the fence in his own striped pyjamas. When it starts to rain, Bruno, Shmuel and other people from the camp are herded into a warm room. As Bruno and Shmuel hold hands, everything goes dark.

About the book

The Boy in the Striped Pyjamas is a heartbreaking story of Auschwitz told through the eyes of a nine-year-old who does not understand what he is seeing. Only the reader (with knowledge) will understand that Bruno's father is the commandant of a concentration camp, that Shmuel is Jewish and that both boys are gassed at the end.

About the teacher's guide

As well as detailed Guided and Shared reading, *Read & Respond: The Boy in the Striped Pyjamas* provides the following activities to cover the English curriculum.

Word reading and spelling

* spelling words with 'ant', 'ent' and 'ough'

Comprehension

* drawing inferences from clues in the text
* describing characters using inference and dialogue
* discussing the theme of friendship
* finding and discussing examples of foreshadowing in the book

Composition

* using expanded noun phrases and ellipsis
* using a thesaurus to improve vocabulary choice
* describing characters with implied information
* researching and writing a biography for Adolf Hitler
* writing a new ending for the story

Speaking and listening

* discussing prejudice and persecution in the novel
* improvising scenes referred to but not described
* exploring the issues of bullying in the story
* researching and presenting information about someone who has spoken out against injustice

Goodnight Mister Tom:

Overview

Topic links

Second World War

Curriculum links

History – Second World War
RE

Text types covered

Information
Letter
Narrative
Playscript

By the same author

Just Henry (Egmont)
Back Home (Puffin)

Alternative books

Carrie's War, by Nina Bawden
(Puffin)

Anne of Green Gables, by LM
Montgomery (Oxford Children's
Classics)

Rooftoppers, by Katherine Rundell
(Faber & Faber)

Plot

Grumpy widower Tom Oakley is allocated evacuee William Beech by the local billeting officer. Willie is terrified, starved and bruised and the only things his mother has sent are the Bible and a belt for Willie to be whipped with. Under Tom's gentle care, Willie gets strong and happy. He learns to read, acts in a play and, for the first time, has friends. However, Willie's peaceful existence is shattered when his mother summons him back home to London. When Tom does not hear from him he travels to London, finds Willie holding a dead baby, locked under the stairs. Eventually Tom is able to adopt Willie. All seems happy for a while until Willie's best friend Zach is killed in the Blitz. In time Willie finds a way to remember Zach with happiness.

About the book

An emotional rollercoaster, *Goodnight Mister Tom* is a deeply moving story of two damaged people healing each other. It deals with very difficult subject matter that might not be appropriate for all children (child abuse, death, and one clear, though healthy reference to sex and Mrs Beech's appalling behaviour while quoting the Bible, will need interpretation). However, the overwhelming message is the restorative power of love (along with good food and exercise).

About the teacher's guide

As well as detailed Guided and Shared reading, *Read & Respond: Goodnight Mister Tom* provides the following activities to cover the English curriculum.

Word reading and spelling
* spelling the suffixes 'able' and 'ible'
* spelling further homophones

Comprehension
* comparing the different settings in the book
* discussing the theme of healing in the book
* investigating the author's use of language
* understanding the historical setting
* discussing the plot structure of the story

Composition
* using modal verbs and the passive voice
* describing new settings
* writing a playscript version

Speaking and listening
* articulating the issues faced by different characters in the book
* speculating about events not described in the story
* improvising new scenes
* giving a presentation about an aspect of the Second World War

Percy Jackson and the Lightning Thief:
Overview

- ### Topic links
  Greek myths

- ### Curriculum links
  History – Ancient Greece
  PSHE

- ### Text types covered
  Information
  Myths
  Narrative
  Poetry
  Instructions
  Letter of application

- ### By the same author
  Percy Jackson and the Sea of Monsters (Puffin)

  Percy Jackson and the Titan's Curse (Puffin)

  The Heroes of Olympus series (Puffin)

  Magnus Chase and the Gods of Asgard series (Puffin)

  Trials of Apollo series (Puffin)

- ### Alternative books
  The Orchard Book of Greek Myths, by Geraldine McCaughrean (Orchard)

  Wolf Brother, by Michelle Paver (Orion)

Plot

Percy Jackson has had a troubled school life; only his friend Grover and teacher Mr Brunner seem to understand him. When a teacher on a field trip turns into a monster and Percy vaporises her, his mother tells him that his father is the god Poseidon. His mother gets him to the safety of Camp Half-Blood but dies in doing so. At the camp he is given a quest to find Zeus's lightning bolt, and with his friends he must track down Hades in the Underworld. He finds the lightning bolt and manages to bring back his mother from the dead at the same time.

About the book

Action all the way with cameos from your favourite Greek gods and heroes, *Percy Jackson and the Lightning Thief* is enormous fun and a great end-of-term book.

About the teacher's guide

As well as detailed Guided and Shared reading, *Read & Respond: Percy Jackson and the Lightning Thief* provides the following activities to cover the English curriculum.

Word reading and spelling
- spelling words with silent letters

Comprehension
- understanding the use of informal language
- picking up clues to make reasonable predictions
- appreciating how the characters create a team
- understanding the structure of a heroic journey plot
- discussing use of the first person, informal narrator
- picking up clues about characters using knowledge of myths

Composition
- using relative clauses and noun phrases
- creating an encyclopaedia of Greek gods and goddesses
- devising instructions for making a mythical call
- writing Grover's letter of application for being a searcher

Speaking and listening
- writing and delivering a dramatic prophecy for Grover
- creating a trailer 'voice-over' for the book
- discussing family relationships and what makes a family
- retelling a Greek myth

Year 6

Curriculum objectives	Charlotte's Web	One Dog and His Boy	Carrie's War	Boy in the Striped Pyjamas	Goodnight Mister Tom	Percy Jackson and the Lightning Thief
Word reading						
To apply their growing knowledge of root words, prefixes and suffixes (etymology and morphology) as listed in English Appendix 1, both to read aloud and to understand the meaning of new words they meet.	✔	✔	✔	✔	✔	✔
Comprehension						
To maintain positive attitudes to reading and understanding of what they read.	✔			✔	✔	
To continue to read and discuss an increasingly wide range of fiction, poetry, plays, non-fiction and reference books or textbooks.						
To read books that are structured in different ways and read for a range of purposes.						
To increase their familiarity with a wide range of books, including myths, legends and traditional stories, modern fiction, fiction from our literary heritage, and books from other cultures and traditions.			✔			✔
To recommend books that they have read to their peers, giving reasons for their choices.				✔	✔	
To identify and discuss themes and conventions in and across a wide range of writing.	✔	✔	✔	✔	✔	
To make comparisons within and across books.				✔	✔	
To learn a wider range of poetry by heart.						
To prepare poems and plays to read aloud and to perform, showing understanding through intonation, tone and volume so that the meaning is clear to an audience.						
To check that the text makes sense to them, discussing their understanding and explaining the meaning of words in context.	✔		✔	✔	✔	✔
To ask questions to improve their understanding of a text.	✔	✔		✔	✔	
To draw inferences such as inferring characters' feelings, thoughts and motives from their actions, and justify inferences with evidence.	✔	✔	✔	✔	✔	✔
To predict what might happen from details stated and implied.			✔			✔
To summarise the main ideas drawn from more than one paragraph, identifying key details that support the main ideas.	✔	✔	✔			✔

Year 6

Curriculum objectives	Charlotte's Web	One Dog and His Boy	Carrie's War	Boy in the Striped Pyjamas	Goodnight Mister Tom	Percy Jackson and the Lightning Thief
To identify how language, structure and presentation contribute to meaning.		✔	✔	✔		
To discuss and evaluate how authors use language, including figurative language, considering the impact on the reader.	✔	✔	✔	✔	✔	✔
To distinguish between statements of fact and opinion.	✔					
To retrieve, record and present information from non-fiction.		✔	✔			
To participate in discussions about books that are read to them and those they can read for themselves, building on their own and others' ideas and challenging views courteously.			✔	✔	✔	
To explain and discuss their understanding of what they have read, including through formal presentations and debates, maintaining a focus on the topic and using notes where necessary.	✔	✔		✔	✔	✔
To provide reasoned justifications for their views.	✔	✔				✔

Transcription: Spelling

	Charlotte's Web	One Dog and His Boy	Carrie's War	Boy in the Striped Pyjamas	Goodnight Mister Tom	Percy Jackson and the Lightning Thief
To use further prefixes and suffixes and understand the guidance for adding them.	✔			✔		
To spell some words with 'silent' letters (for example, knight, psalm, solemn).				✔		✔
To continue to distinguish between homophones and other words which are often confused.					✔	✔
To use knowledge of morphology and etymology in spelling and understand that the spelling of some words needs to be learned specifically, as listed in English Appendix 1.		✔	✔		✔	✔
To use dictionaries to check the spelling and meaning of words.						✔
To use the first three or four letters of a word to check spelling, meaning or both of these in a dictionary.						
To use a thesaurus.				✔	✔	✔

Handwriting

To write legibly, fluently and with increasing speed.						

Curriculum objectives	Charlotte's Web	One Dog and His Boy	Carrie's War	Boy in the Striped Pyjamas	Goodnight Mister Tom	Percy Jackson and the Lightning Thief
To choose which shape of a letter to use when given choices and decide whether or not to join specific letters.						
To choose the writing implement that is best suited for a task.						
Composition						
To identify the audience for and purpose of the writing, selecting the appropriate form and using other similar writing as models for their own.	✔	✔	✔	✔	✔	✔
To note and develop initial ideas, drawing on reading and research where necessary.		✔	✔	✔		
In writing narratives, to consider how authors have developed characters and settings in what pupils have read, listened to or seen performed.	✔		✔			✔
To select appropriate grammar and vocabulary, understanding how such choices can change and enhance meaning.	✔			✔	✔	✔
In narratives, to describe settings, characters and atmosphere and integrate dialogue to convey character and advance the action.	✔	✔	✔	✔		✔
To précis longer passages.		✔		✔	✔	✔
To use a wide range of devices to build cohesion within and across paragraphs.	✔			✔	✔	
To use further organisational and presentational devices to structure text and to guide the reader (for example, headings, bullet points, underlining).	✔		✔			✔
To assess the effectiveness of their own and others' writing.			✔	✔	✔	
To propose changes to vocabulary, grammar and punctuation to enhance effects and clarify meaning.				✔	✔	
To ensure the consistent and correct use of tense throughout a piece of writing.					✔	
To ensure correct subject and verb agreement when using singular and plural, distinguishing between the language of speech and writing and choosing the appropriate register.						
To proofread for spelling and punctuation errors.					✔	
To perform their own compositions, using appropriate intonation, volume, and movement so that meaning is clear.	✔	✔		✔	✔	

Curriculum objectives	Charlotte's Web	One Dog and His Boy	Carrie's War	Boy in the Striped Pyjamas	Goodnight Mister Tom	Percy Jackson and the Lightning Thief
Composition: Grammar, vocabulary and punctuation						
To recognise vocabulary and structures that are appropriate for formal speech and writing, including subjunctive forms.	✓					✓
To use passive verbs to affect the presentation of information in a sentence.		✓	✓		✓	
To use the perfect form of verbs to mark relationships of time and cause.						
To use expanded noun phrases to convey complicated information concisely.				✓		✓
To use modal verbs or adverbs to indicate degrees of possibility.	✓		✓		✓	
To use relative clauses beginning with 'who', 'which', 'where', 'when', 'whose', 'that' or with an implied (omitted) relative pronoun.		✓				✓
To learn the grammar for Year 6 in English Appendix 2.	✓	✓	✓	✓	✓	✓
To use commas to clarify meaning or avoid ambiguity in writing.	✓	✓				
To use hyphens to avoid ambiguity.			✓			
To use brackets, dashes or commas to indicate parenthesis.			✓	✓		
To use semi-colons, colons or dashes to mark boundaries between independent clauses.	✓		✓		✓	
To use a colon to introduce a list.		✓				✓
To punctuate bullet points consistently.	✓	✓				
To use and understand the grammatical terminology in English Appendix 2 accurately and appropriately in discussing their writing and reading.		✓				
Spoken language						
To listen and respond appropriately to adults and their peers.			✓			
To ask relevant questions to extend their understanding and knowledge.					✓	✓

Year 6

Curriculum objectives	Charlotte's Web	One Dog and His Boy	Carrie's War	Boy in the Striped Pyjamas	Goodnight Mister Tom	Percy Jackson and the Lightning Thief
To use relevant strategies to build their vocabulary.						
To articulate and justify answers, arguments and opinions.	✓	✓	✓	✓		
To give well-structured descriptions, explanations and narratives for different purposes, including for expressing feelings.	✓	✓	✓	✓	✓	✓
To maintain attention and participate actively in collaborative conversations, staying on topic and initiating and responding to comments.		✓				
To use spoken language to develop understanding through speculating, hypothesising, imagining and exploring ideas.	✓	✓	✓		✓	
To speak audibly and fluently with an increasing command of Standard English.						
To participate in discussions, presentations, performances, role play, improvisations and debates.	✓	✓	✓	✓	✓	✓
To gain, maintain and monitor the interest of the listeners.	✓					
To consider and evaluate different viewpoints, attending to and building on the contributions of others.			✓			
To select and use appropriate registers for effective communication.						

Suggested programme of study

	Year 1			Year 2		
	Suggested title	Title by the same author	Alternative books	Suggested title	Title by the same author	Alternative books
Autumn Term 1	• Jasper's Beanstalk	• Tales from Percy's Park • Stories Jesus Told • Thud • Albert le Blanc • Q Pootle 5	• The Tiny Seed, by Eric Carle • 'Jack and the Beanstalk' • Oliver's Vegetables, by Vivian French	• Oliver's Vegetables	• Oliver's Fruit Salad • Oliver's Milkshake • Yucky Worms	• Jasper's Beanstalk, by Nick Butterworth • I Will Not Ever Never Eat a Tomato, by Lauren Child
Autumn Term 2	• Owl Babies	• Can't You Sleep, Little Bear? • Farmer Duck • The Pig in the Pond	• The Owl Who Was Afraid of the Dark, by Jill Tomlinson • Where's My Teddy? by Jez Alborough	• Stick Man	• The Gruffalo • Room on the Broom • Tiddler • Zog • A Squash and a Squeeze	• Unfortunately, by Alan Durant • Tiddler, by Julia Donaldson
Spring Term 1	• We're Going on a Bear Hunt	• Michael Rosen's Sad Book • Mustard, Custard, Grumble Belly and Gravy • Little Rabbit Foo Foo	• Bears in the Night, by Stan and Jan Berenstain • Whatever Next! by Jill Murphy	• Aliens Love Underpants	• Monster Max's Shark Spaghetti • Monsters Love Underpants • Superkid • Spider Sandwiches	• Pants, by Giles Andreae • Beegu, by Alexis Deacon • Man on the Moon, by Simon Bartram
Spring Term 2	• Zog	• The Gruffalo • Room on the Broom • Tiddler • Stick Man • Superworm • A Squash and a Squeeze	• George and the Dragon, by Christopher Wormell • The Paper Bag Princess, by Robert Munsch • Princess Smartypants, by Babette Cole	• Room on the Broom	• The Gruffalo • Stick Man • Tiddler • Zog • A Squash and a Squeeze	• The Smartest Giant in Town, by Julia Donaldson • A Squash and a Squeeze, by Julia Donaldson
Summer Term 1	• Handa's Surprise	• Handa's Hen	• Oliver's Vegetables, by Vivian French • Rosie's Walk, by Pat Hutchins • Don't Forget the Bacon! by Pat Hutchins	• The Lighthouse Keeper's Lunch	• The Lighthouse Keeper's New Friend • The Lighthouse Keeper's Breakfast • The Lighthouse Keeper's Picnic • Small Knight and George	• The Mousehole Cat, by Antonia Barber • Winnie at the Seaside, by Valerie Thomas
Summer Term 2	• Superworm	• The Gruffalo • Room on the Broom • Tiddler • Stick Man • What the Ladybird Heard • Tyrannosaurus Drip • A Squash and a Squeeze	• Stick Man, by Julia Donaldson	• Winnie the Witch	• Winnie at the Seaside • Winnie's Midnight Dragon • Winnie's Magic Wand • Winnie's Amazing Pumpkin	• Meg and Mog, by Helen Nicoll • The Worst Witch, by Jill Murphy • Elmer, by David McKee

	Year 3			Year 4		
	Suggested title	Title by the same author	Alternative books	Suggested title	Title by the same author	Alternative books
Autumn Term 1	• Bill's New Frock	• The Diary of a Killer Cat • Flour Babies • Goggle-eyes • The Angel of Nitshill Road • Madame Doubtfire	• Princess Smartypants, by Babette Cole • The Diary of a Killer Cat, by Anne Fine	• George's Marvellous Medicine	• The BFG • Danny the Champion of the World • Charlie and the Chocolate Factory • Matilda • The Twits • The Enormous Crocodile	• The Twits, by Roald Dahl
Autumn Term 2	• The Owl Who Was Afraid of the Dark	• The Penguin Who Wanted to Find Out • The Otter Who Wanted to Know • The Hen Who Wouldn't Give Up • The Cat Who Wanted to Go Home	• Owl Babies, by Martin Waddell • The Owl Who Was Afraid of the Dark, abridged picture book version	• Why the Whales Came	• The Wreck of the Zanzibar • Kensuke's Kingdom • War Horse • The Butterfly Lion • Private Peaceful • The Amazing Story of Adolphus Tips	• Katie Morag and the Two Grandmothers, by Mairi Hedderwick • Kensuke's Kingdom, by Michael Morpurgo
Spring Term 1	• The Twits	• The BFG • Danny the Champion of the World • Charlie and the Chocolate Factory • Matilda • George's Marvellous Medicine • The Enormous Crocodile	• The Enormous Crocodile, by Roald Dahl • You're a Bad Man, Mr Gum! by Andy Stanton	• Stig of the Dump	• The Town that Went South • Me and my Million • The Night the Water Came	• Skellig, by David Almond • The Iron Man, by Ted Hughes • Why the Whales Came, by Michael Morpurgo • Mr Stink, by David Walliams
Spring Term 2	• The Iron Man	• The Iron Woman • How the Whale Became and Other Stories	• The Selfish Giant, by Oscar Wilde • 'The Lion and the Mouse', by Aesop • Wendel's Workshop, by Chris Riddell	• Hetty Feather	• Katy • The Suitcase Kid • Further stories about Hetty Feather (Sapphire Battersea, Emerald Star, Diamond, Little Stars)	• Cliffhanger, by Jacqueline Wilson • Street Child, by Berlie Doherty • A Little Princess, by Frances Hodgson Burnett
Summer Term 1	• Diary of a Wimpy Kid	• Diary of a Wimpy Kid: Rodrick Rules • Diary of a Wimpy Kid: The Last Straw • Diary of a Wimpy Kid: Dog Days • Diary of a Wimpy Kid: The Ugly Truth	• Bill's New Frock, by Anne Fine • Captain Underpants, by Dav Pilkey	• Millions	• The Astounding Broccoli Boy • Framed • Cosmic • Sputnik's Guide to Life on Earth	• Billionaire Boy, by David Walliams • The Boy in the Dress, by David Walliams
Summer Term 2	• Danny the Champion of the World	• The BFG • Charlie and the Chocolate Factory • Matilda • George's Marvellous Medicine • The Enormous Crocodile	• The Enormous Crocodile, by Roald Dahl • George's Marvellous Medicine, by Roald Dahl	• How to Train Your Dragon	• That Rabbit Belongs to Emily Brown • Hiccup the Viking Who Was Seasick	• The Saga of Erik the Viking, by Terry Jones • Hiccup the Viking Who Was Seasick, by Cressida Cowell • Diary of a Wimpy Kid, by Jeff Kinney

	Year 5			Year 6		
	Suggested title	Title by the same author	Alternative books	Suggested title	Title by the same author	Alternative books
Autumn Term 1	• Kensuke's Kingdom	• War Horse • Why the Whales Came • The Wreck of the Zanzibar • Private Peaceful	• Why the Whales Came, by Michael Morpurgo • The Great Kapok Tree, by Lynne Cherry	• Charlotte's Web	• Stuart Little	• The Owl Who Was Afraid of the Dark, by Jill Tomlinson • The Sheep-Pig, by Dick King-Smith
Autumn Term 2	• Charlie and the Chocolate Factory	• The BFG • Danny the Champion of the World • George's Marvellous Medicine • Matilda • The Twits • The Enormous Crocodile	• George's Marvellous Medicine, by Roald Dahl	• One Dog and His Boy	• Journey to the River Sea • The Secret of Platform 13 • The Star of Kazan • The Dragonfly Pool	• The World According to Humphrey, by Betty G Birney
Spring Term 1	• Varjak Paw	• The Outlaw Varjak Paw • Phoenix	• Gobbolino the Witch's Cat, by Ursula Moray Williams • I Was a Rat, by Philip Pullman • The Owl Who Was Afraid of the Dark, by Jill Tomlinson	• Carrie's War	• The Peppermint Pig	• The Lion and the Unicorn, by Shirley Hughes • War Boy, by Michael Foreman
Spring Term 2	• Holes	• There's a Boy in the Girls' Bathroom • Small Steps	• The Diary of a Killer Cat, by Anne Fine	• The Boy in the Striped Pyjamas	• The Terrible Thing that Happened to Barnaby Brocket • Stay Where You Are and Then Leave	• The Mozart Question, by Michael Morpurgo • The Terrible Thing that Happened to Barnaby Brocket, by John Boyne • The Silver Sword, by Ian Serraillier • I am David, by Anne Holm
Summer Term 1	• The Amazing Maurice and His Educated Rodents	• The Colour of Magic • The Wee Free Men • A Hat Full of Sky • I Shall Wear Midnight	• Truckers, by Terry Pratchett • Igraine the Brave, by Cornelia Funke	• Goodnight Mister Tom	• Just Henry • Back Home	• Carrie's War, by Nina Bawden • Anne of Green Gables, by LM Montgomery • Rooftoppers, by Katherine Rundell
Summer Term 2	• War Horse	• Private Peaceful • Farm Boy • An Eagle in the Snow • The Mozart Question	• War Game, by Michael Foreman • Why the Whales Came, by Michael Morpurgo	• Percy Jackson and the Lightning Thief	• Percy Jackson and the Sea of Monsters • Percy Jackson and the Titan's Curse • The Heroes of Olympus series • Magnus Chase and the Gods of Asgard series • Trials of Apollo series	• The Orchard Book of Greek Myths, by Geraldine McCaughrean • Wolf Brother, by Michelle Paver

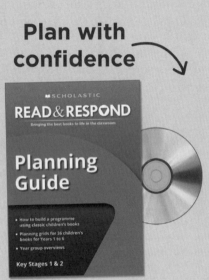
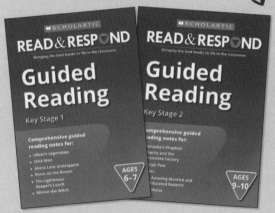